Starting with the
SHOPPER
Research Insights for
Winning at Retail

Scott Young is the President of Perception Research Services (www.prsresearch.com), a company that conducts over 800 research studies each year to help companies understand shoppers, ensure packaging excellence, and "win at retail." In additional to serving clients such as Unilever, AB InBev, and MARS, Scott is the author of *Winning at Retail: Insights from 35 Years of Packaging and Shopper Research* and a contributor to publications such as *Brand Packaging, Quirk's Marketing Research*, the *Design Management Journal*, and *Shopper Marketing*. Scott also speaks regularly at marketing research and design conferences and guest lectures at universities including Wharton and Notre Dame.

Starting with the
SHOPPER

Research Insights for Winning at Retail

SCOTT YOUNG

Perception Research Services

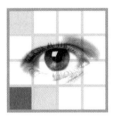

Paramount Market Publishing, Inc.

Paramount Market Publishing, Inc.
950 Danby Road, Suite 136
Ithaca, NY 14850
www.paramountbooks.com
Voice: 607-275-8100; 888-787-8100   Fax: 607-275-8101

Publisher: James Madden
Editorial Director: Doris Walsh

Cataloging in Publication Data available

ISBN-10: 1-941688-23-3 | ISBN-13: 978-1-941688-23-6

Contents

Preface   vii

Chapter 1   Making the Case for Design   1
             Using Research to Document the Impact of Packaging

Chapter 2   Understanding the Shopper Journey   10
             In-Store Insights for Enhancing Shopper Marketing

Chapter 3   In the Home & On the Shelf   19
             Gathering Insights to Promote New Product Success

Chapter 4   Bringing Eye-Tracking to the Store   24
             Applications, Observations & Shopper Insights

Chapter 5   Focusing on the Two Moments of Truth   31
             Uncovering the Drivers of Success & Disaster

Chapter 6   Winning the Battle at the Shelf   38
             Competing Effectively against Private Label Brands

Chapter 7   Breaking Through the Clutter   45
             Strategies for Success in a World of "Too Much Choice"

Chapter 8   Improving the Screening Process   51
             Avoiding Missteps & Identifying the Strongest New Concepts

Chapter 9   Getting the Message Right   59
             Insights for Effective On-Pack Messaging

Chapter 10   Investing in Success   66
              5 Best Practices for Effective Packaging Research

Chapter 11   Improving Success Rates & ROI   74
              Avoiding 5 Common Mistakes

Chapter 12   Doing Simple Design Well   81
              Leveraging the Power of Clarity & Simplicity

Chapter 13   Packaging & In-Market Impact   86
              Optimizing the Rollout of New Packaging Systems

Chapter 14   Brands Without Borders   92
              Strategies for Effective Global Design

Chapter 15   How is China Different?   97
              Insights for Connecting with the Chinese Shopper

Chapter 16   Getting the Most from Eye-Tracking   103
              Understanding Its Applications, Insights & Limitations

Chapter 17   Getting to Why   111
              Measuring Emotion in Packaging Research

Chapter 18   Making Packaging Work Online   117
              Linking the Digital & Physical Shopping Experiences

Chapter 19   Connecting with Hispanic Shoppers   121
              New Insights from Eye-Tracking Research

Acknowledgments   128

Preface

Starting with the Shopper is our second book, following *Winning at Retail,* which was published in 2010. Both are compilations of "white papers" that my colleagues at PRS and I have written on a regular basis, in response to the key issues, questions, and challenges raised by our clients.

In reviewing and organizing these items, I was struck by two themes.

The first was the breadth of new topics addressed over the past five years, including Emotional Measurement, In-Store Mobile Eye-Tracking, and Web-Based Shopping. These issues reflect a rapidly changing world, which constantly presents our clients with new challenges and new tools and technologies for gathering insights.

The second was the continuity of several core challenges and effective strategies that we've seen since PRS began our research back in the early 1970s. These include the struggle to "break through" and connect with shoppers in a cluttered world, and to ensure that packaging and shopper marketing are fully understood and valued by senior management. Similarly, we've continually seen the value of clarity and simplicity at the "first moment of truth" and the importance of speaking with shoppers at the outset of initiatives, rather than waiting for last-minute testing.

I take comfort in this dichotomy. To me, it suggests that as new situations arrive, we can find valuable guidance and direction from "lessons learned" from experience. And in fact, this idea links directly to the primary objective of this book: **To distill and share PRS' learning from over 40 years of packaging and shopper research.**

[handwritten margin notes: "what about online, social, Amazon, mobile, showrooming, etc? all this shopper + retail stuff is still important but it's only a portion of the modern customer experience."]

[handwritten note: "most of this book seems to be FMCG?"]

Through these chapters, I've attempted to share "best practices" that we've seen work across categories and countries, in a manner that will help you to find commonalities and apply them to your own challenges. Indeed, my hope and intent is that this book can serve as an ongoing resource, which will provide a foundation, and perhaps help spark your thinking, as you begin a new initiative.

On a final note, I'm always eager to continue the dialogue and hear about your new challenges, so please feel free reach out to me at syoung@prsresearch.com and look for our new articles at www.prsresearch.com.

SCOTT

Making the Case for Design

Using Research to Document the Impact of Packaging

As marketers, designers, and engineers, we all face a common challenge: How do we persuade senior management to invest in packaging? Many of us know from experience that this is often an uphill battle as organizations weigh tangible costs and perceived risks against uncertain returns. In addition, pack innovation often runs against the deeply ingrained caution of individual executives who may feel that they have been burned in the past.

Packaging has a direct and measurable impact on purchase decisions and in-market sales.

On a broader level, packaging is also fighting for attention and resources against other (and perhaps "hotter" or "sexier") marketing vehicles such as advertising and web marketing. While most companies have moved beyond thinking of packaging solely as a container and cost center, it is still apt to be overlooked and underfunded as a marketing vehicle and source of competitive advantage. With that thought in mind, we'll review strategies for making the case for packaging investment and share evidence and prospective gathered from our many years of packaging research.

The Many Roles of Packaging

In our experience, many discussions and requests for funding begin with familiar statements regarding the centrality of packaging in both the shopping and usage experience:

- Packaging is the brand's spokesperson at the first moment of truth (in-store), where most purchase decisions are made.

- Packaging is the embodiment of the brand and is prominently featured in nearly all forms of marketing communication (TV, web, and print).

- Packaging is often part of the product usage experience and can have a significant impact on both consumer satisfaction and usage frequency.

In addition, there is a strong argument to be made that packaging is more important than ever:

The fragmentation of mass media and fewer people viewing TV ads lead to more in-store decision-making.

The reality of increasing clutter or product proliferation ("more choice") makes it more difficult to break through and differentiate.

The growth and improvement of private label puts more pressure on national brands to justify price premiums.

Yet while these points are true and quite compelling, they also suffer from being somewhat abstract. In order to persuade, they need to be brought to life and, ideally, quantified.

The growth and improvement of private label brands is making packaging more important than ever before.

Success Stories (and Disasters)

Fortunately, finding tangible examples of the power of packaging is not all that difficult. However, the challenge is that the "disasters" often resonate most clearly in marketers' minds. For example, Tropicana's missteps, in which an ill-fated change in pack graphics led immediately to double-digit sales declines and millions in foregone sales, were perhaps the most publicized packaging story of the past decade. And indeed, many companies have their own cautionary tale of a packaging initiative gone wrong, leading to confusion at the shelf and sales drops. This is unfortunate and problematic, as the primary takeaway for many senior managers is that packaging changes are inherently risky. Rather than illustrating the power of packaging, negative examples are more likely to instill fear and, thus, serve as an excuse for avoiding investment.

On the positive side, there are numerous case studies of packaging driving business growth in many ways, including:

- Brands rooted in compelling, differentiated or iconic packaging. Examples include method, Fructis, Special K, Coca-Cola, and Pringles.

- Unique packaging as an integral component of successful new brands or product lines: think U by Kotex, Colgate Optic White, MiO, and Gevalia.

- New packaging graphics driving sales increases or revitalizing well-established brands such as Renuzit, Kraft Macaroni & Cheese, and Miller Lite.

- New packaging forms growing product categories and increasing product consumption including On-the-Go, Fridge, and 100 Calorie packs.

However, the challenge is that isolating the role and positive impact of packaging can often be difficult. Pack changes rarely happen in isolation, and thus, success may well be attributed to other marketing vehicles, product, pricing, promotion, etc. While packaging is often a foundational and necessary element of new product success, it is inevitably one piece of a larger effort.

Recently we've made progress in isolating and quantifying the role of packaging in new product success. Through joint research with BASES, we've documented the linkage between great packaging and in-market sales and integrated packaging in our formulas to arrive at more accurate volume forecasting. Thus, we can now begin to quantify the dollar value of exceptional new product packaging, which is an important step to justifying investment.

Getting to the Numbers

How can we talk about packaging and pack investment in a manner that speaks to senior management and their CFOs? One answer involves moving beyond abstract arguments and anecdotal case studies and reaching toward their language of numbers and ROI.

It's here that shopper research can provide an answer, by helping to quantify the upside potential associated with new packaging. Specifically, research can gauge and isolate the impact of a new packaging system on shoppers' purchase decisions at the shelf, the single most direct and validated measure of in-market sales and potential financial return.

By simulating the introduction of new packaging on full shelves (and holding pricing and other factors constant), we're able to see whether or not packaging alone influences brand choice or drives incremental purchases. And across thousands of studies, this research has revealed some interesting evidence regarding the power of packaging: Typically, the "sales gap" between the strongest and the weakest packaging system tested is approximately 5 percent of shoppers.

For example, 30 percent of shoppers may purchase the brand with a new package on the shelf, while only 25 percent purchase the same brand with its current pack on the same shelf. While this figure may not seem high at first, the reality is that a 5 percent gain in market share is actually enormous: For a brand with $100 million in sales, a successful new package can translate to $5 million or more in increased sales.

> In many of our studies, we find that packaging changes alone drive even more pronounced positive or negative changes in purchase levels.

These dramatic success stories are most common with smaller brands, which are often overlooked on shelf and have the greatest upside potential from more impactful packaging. Conversely, the "disasters averted" often involve larger, well-established brands, which have higher downside risk of confusing or alienating current buyers.

> In over half of our studies, we find that new packaging systems have a significant positive impact on brand imagery, packaging functionality, or product usage.

While these metrics typically have a less immediate impact on sales, they speak to the longer-term influence of packaging on brand building and user satisfaction.

How does controlled pre-testing research of this nature translate to the real world? The connection is real and validated, but inevitably, in-market performance is also impacted by many other factors, including soft rollouts, POS support, pricing changes, etc. In fact, our analysis of study results versus actual sales strongly suggests that how a new packaging system is rolled out can dramatically impact its in-market performance. Thus, marketers need to focus on effective follow-through, in order to ensure that great new packaging translates to in-market success and a positive ROI.

Four Best Practices for Documenting Packaging's Value

So what can we do to make the case for packaging more effectively? Here are several best practices to integrate within the packaging development and research process.

1. Start with your current packaging (to document the need for change)

vs.
"Coca-Cola"

By benchmarking current packaging relative to competition and to incoming brand imagery (name only), marketers can help determine if pack changes are advisable.

Typically, research (particularly quantitative, numerical research) has been used to assess and "sell-in" new packaging systems prior to launch. However, a growing number of companies are periodically benchmarking the performance of their current packaging, relative to both competition and incoming brand imagery (based on name only). Often, the results are eye-opening, as we've found many cases in which well-established brands are actually selling despite their packaging rather than because of it. This proactive approach can be used:

- To allocate resources to the brands in the greatest need and help avoid unnecessary and misguided design changes.

- To set meaningful design objectives which can then translate into clear action standards.

In fact, we've seen that pre-design research of this nature consistently leads to higher success rates for new design systems in our studies and in-market. That's because it helps ensure that redesign efforts are solving the real problem rather than reacting to misguided assumptions or subjective preferences.

2. Simulate the introduction of new packaging (to forecast sales impact)

When testing new design systems, simulating the introduction of a new package within the competitive context—and measuring its impact on brand choice—is the most accurate way to gauge the in-market impact of a new packaging system. Generally speaking, the more realistic the packaging and competitive context (ideally, a full life-size shelf with pricing, replicating a retail channel), the more predictive a study will be.

Conversely, when we ask people to compare options for the same brand (*Which of these five different packs would you prefer for this brand?*), it encourages them to think like art directors or brand managers rather than shoppers. In fact, we've found that direct comparisons between packaging graphics or structures (Design A versus B) lead shoppers to dramatically overstate their preferences. Thus, marketers may walk away thinking they've hit a home run, when the new pack would actually do little to move the needle. Similarly, here is a list of questions that it is best to avoid asking, as they consistently generate misleading responses:

- *Would you see this pack on shelf?*
- *Would you notice this pack change?*
- *Would you find this confusing?*
- *Would you pay more for this feature?*
- *Would this pack lead you to use the product more?*

New packaging structures and delivery systems can make a difference on shelf, in the hand and in the home.

3. Test new packs from the shelf to the home (to measure their full value)

When testing changes in pack structure, it is ideal to fully replicate the consumer's experience from the purchase decision through product usage. That's because a new pack can have a positive impact on many levels:

- On shelf (in enhancing visibility and facilitating shopping)
- In the hand (improving product perceptions, brand imagery, or price/value)
- In the home (improving functionality or driving increased usage)

If studies focus solely on one dimension (such as communication or functionality), they risk short-changing the true added-value of a pack innovation. Thus, they may lead to the mistaken conclusion that a new feature or delivery system won't be worth the investment.

Holistic testing also makes sense for many new products, as we've found that packaging has a direct impact on product perceptions and consumer satisfaction. Shoppers often form their expectations based on the pack, and these impressions form their baseline in judging a new product. Thus, blind testing of new products without packaging can be quite misleading if there is a disconnect between packaging communication and product delivery.

4. Track in-market performance to uncover success drivers and develop new case studies

Designers and engineers are well-served to consistently track what happens after new packaging systems are introduced to market. Certainly, this can be challenging, given the complexity of sales data and many factors in play. However, there are ways to minimize confusion and help clarify the link between packaging and performance:

- Use lead retail partners or channels to pilot new packaging systems.
- Invest in clean or hard rollouts of new packaging.

- Systematically document the key factors accompanying pack introductions.

By following these processes, creating a continuous feedback loop, and possibly linking to market modeling efforts, companies can learn from experience and build knowledge regarding the drivers of success in their categories. In addition, marketers and designers will be rewarded with very relevant and quantified case studies illustrating the power of packaging within their organization.

Making the Case for Design

A small but growing number of business leaders truly grasp the power of design and have elevated its role and resources within their organizations. They understand that packaging is a powerful marketing vehicle rather than a cost center—and that the right pack changes can drive millions in sales. However, these leaders remain the exception rather than the rule. In most companies, packaging must continually struggle for resources and investment and is under constant pressure to prove its worth.

Research and sales data can help us make this case by serving as a bridge between the world of packaging design and that of senior management. Specifically, they can identify the right opportunities—and most importantly, document and quantify the value of packaging innovation in a language that speaks to executives and retail partners. Thus, marketers, designers and engineers are well advised to embrace the numbers as a tool to demonstrate the value of their work and make the case for continued investment in packaging.

Understanding the Shopper Journey
In-Store Insights for Enhancing Shopper Marketing

To guide shopper marketing, we need to understand which purchase decisions take place in the aisle.

Each year, PRS pre-tests several hundred new packaging systems, prior to their introduction in market. And we've long emphasized the shelf context, because we've learned and validated that on-shelf performance (brand visibility and shop-ability) links directly to in-market sales.

More recently, we've also been encouraging clients to think beyond the shelf and to "start with the shopper" as they develop new packaging. In fact, we now begin many initiatives with in-store studies, to observe shopping behavior (via *PRS Mobile Eye-Tracking*), document engagement with POS materials and uncover the dynamics of different retail environments. In this chapter, we'll share some of what we've seen and learned, and discuss implications for improving packaging and shopper marketing.

Understanding the Shopper & Store

Shopper understanding is clearly an important foundation for effective packaging and in-store marketing. However, there's a potentially over-whelming amount of information that can be gathered about shoppers, from demographic profiles to "decision trees" and segmentations. And while much of this data can be valuable, we've found it helpful to focus on a central question:

Which purchase decisions are we most likely to influence in the aisle?

We've found that the answer varies widely across brands, categories, and countries. In some cases, the main opportunity at retail lies in winning over brand switchers or driving impulse purchases. However, for many well-established brands, the most viable path to profitability rests in driving incremental purchases /or trade-up from brand loyalists. The key is to understand this dynamic for your brand, and to use it to shape in-store strategy, including packaging, merchandising, and product innovation. When a brand's core in-store objective is focused, it becomes far easier to develop clear design briefs, communication hierarchies, and creative strategies.

Across many in-store studies, we've also found that it is important to observe and emphasize *behavior* ("what shoppers do") rather than relying upon *claimed* shopping patterns, preferences or priorities ("what shoppers say"). That's because in the midst of hundreds of SKUs and stimuli overload, shoppers are often on "auto-pilot," and their decisions are often driven by what gets seen (and missed). In fact, in a recent study in a food category, we found that shoppers typically spent under a minute in the aisle and levels of comparison shopping were remarkably low (about 5 percent). *PRS Mobile Eye-Tracking* also revealed a deeper insight: Rather than finding "their brand," shoppers were selecting the first brand (presumably from a set of "acceptable brands") that met their primary criteria (flavor, form, etc.). The implication was clear: In this category (as in many impulse and habitual categories), the first priority was to visually "preempt" competition through packaging, shelving, or displays.

It is difficult to separate the shopper and the store, because shopper profiles, missions, and behavior vary widely by retail channel. For example, customers purchasing beverages in a convenience store have a very different profile than those buying in a mass or club store: They are buying different sizes, for different usage occasions, and with different decision criteria. The retail environments themselves also vary widely, as they have unique "retail realities" (in terms of lighting, shelving and merchandising) that impact how shoppers encounter packaging. For example, a brand may be positioned on the bottom shelf at one retailer—and thus the top panels or caps will have to do the "heavy lifting" in terms of brand and product communication. In another channel, bright overhead lighting may create havoc on shiny packages, rendering them nearly unreadable. Of course, it's not feasible to customize packaging for each retailer or every challenge. However, by doing in-store "homework" in advance, we can identify and mitigate these issues. Specifically, we can encourage clients to "design for the worst case scenario" and to develop new packaging and merchandising systems that limit the potential for disaster.

Optimizing Packaging & In-Store Marketing

Packaging and point-of-sale materials clearly need to work together to facilitate shopping and drive purchase. Thus, our in-store research often centers on documenting shoppers' engagement with displays, signage,

Strong in-store displays work from the ground up and connect with shoppers on an emotional level.

and packaging, and in uncovering the roles of the different "touch-points" along the path-to-purchase. And across countries, categories and retailers, several patterns have consistently emerged.

There's no question that a great deal of Point-of-Sale (POS) investment is wasted.

Often, that's due to poor store placement. In a recent beverage study in the U.S. and Argentina, *PRS Eye-Tracking* revealed that not a single shopper (of the over 100 people we observed) looked upward to engage with overhead promotional signage. This finding is largely consistent with our experience across studies: Shoppers use ceiling-based materials to guide store navigation, but once they are in the aisle, their focus is straight ahead or slightly downward. Thus, point-of-sale materials at eye-level or arm-level (interspersed with packaging) are far more visually impactful than materials positioned above the products.

If displays are too complex, they're very likely to be ignored.

In other cases, we've found that excessive in-store merchandising overwhelms shoppers, rather than helping them. In a recent study for a technology marketer (across several retail channels), we uncovered that over 85 percent of shoppers engaged with product displays and fact tags, but other materials (including comparison charts and selector guides) were consistently ignored (under 15 percent visibility), and most likely represented a waste of resources. As a result, the marketer re-designed some materials and eliminated others, leading to an easier shopping experience.

Packaging and POS materials typically have different strengths, "profiles" and roles in the shopping process.

Displays and signage can be valuable in creating visibility and attention (particularly for smaller brands)—and in helping brands to create a "beacon" or destination in the aisle. They can also be very effective in driving impulse purchase, particularly when coupled with a price/value message. And given their size, displays can also present an opportunity to connect more emotionally and viscerally with shoppers, often through visual imagery that links to users and usage occasions. However, one very important guideline is to keep it simple, via a compelling image or a quick message.

When POS gets complex, it is almost always ignored.

In fact, when we've tested POS systems designed to compare products, facilitate shopping or drive trade-up, the results have nearly always been disappointing because shoppers typically rely on packaging for product comparisons.

These findings suggest that packaging and POS have somewhat different "profiles" and optimal applications:

- POS materials can be viewed as closer to an extension of advertising, in terms of its ability to drive awareness or attention, to create an emotional connection, and convey a single key message.

- Packaging, as the embodiment of the product, is somewhat more factual and "rational" in its nature. As shoppers get closer to their actual purchase decision, they are looking for key information and reassurance, i.e., *Am I buying the right product?*

- We've found that marketers (including retailers) have an opportunity to significantly improve their point-of-sale efforts by keeping a few simple, tactical principles in mind:

- Work from the Floor Up *(Not the Ceiling Down)*
- Keep It Simple
- Connect Emotionally
- Surprise & Delight *(via Unique Design)*
- Facilitate Shopping *(Don't Impede It!)*

And while this last point might be self-evident, our research suggests that it is frequently ignored. We repeatedly come across situations in which signage obscures packaging and thus limits information delivery. In a recent study, *PRS Eye-Tracking* revealed that shoppers were actively avoiding POS stickers on freezer doors, in their efforts to "find" the products/packages behind them. Shelf blades were far more effective, as they drew attention and helped shoppers navigate the aisle—and didn't block shoppers' view of packaging, once they reached their area of focus and began actively considering products.

Leveraging Shelf-Ready Packaging

The growth of shelf-ready or retail-ready packaging (SRP) has highlighted many of these issues, as it represents the intersection of packaging and POS communication. SRPs (secondary packaging display cartons) are very common in Europe, particularly in fast-growing discount channels—and they've been promoted by some retailers and channels in the U.S., primarily due to efficiencies in stocking. However, one trip to the store reveals that SRP can significantly impact a brand's in-store presentation, for better or worse:

If shelf-ready packaging is not designed properly, it can compromise in-store communication.

- If leveraged properly, SRP can effectively serve as a display and help drive visibility, facilitate shop-ability and/or convey an important brand message.

- If not, SRP can end up significantly compromising packaging communication, by blocking its visibility or accessibility, or leading to poor package orientation, e.g., knocked over packs.

To maximize positive outcomes, the most important principle is to design the SRP to complement the packaging, by focusing on a specific communication objective. For example, if a brand family is relatively complex, the SRP may provide an excellent opportunity to facilitate shop-ability, perhaps via calling out specific varieties or sub-brands. Or if small dimensions limit the opportunity for on-pack communication, an SRP may be best utilized to convey a clear, differentiating, and motivating brand message, i.e., a reason-to-believe. And of course, part of "complementing the packaging" is designing the SRP to properly highlight and orient the packaging, even when many packs have been sold and the display is only half-full.

From Packaging to "Winning at Retail"

So what does "starting with the shopper" really mean? And how can companies consistently apply shopper-focused insights to improve their packaging and in-store marketing? Here are several "best practices" that we've seen make a difference.

Building the Shopper (& Store) into Design Briefs

Too often, packaging briefs are largely excerpts from brand positioning statements and advertising efforts, focused almost entirely on communication. To shift this mindset, additional components should be built in to incorporate shopper understanding (most notably, decision making processes and priorities at the shelf) and "retail realities" (competitive set, lighting, shelving, etc.). This can help ensure that packaging is designed with specific retail challenges and shopper-based objectives in mind.

Integrating Packaging, SRP & POS Design

Many companies have internal "silos" (between sales and marketing, shopper and brand, packaging and signage, etc.) that lead to materials being created in isolation. To move forward, companies need to more broadly think, design, and, ideally, organize, around the larger vision of "optimizing in-store marketing." At a minimum, design efforts should start with both a strategic and tactical understanding of how packaging and POS will work together: Designers need to know the roles of each vehicle—and to anticipate how the presence of signage and displays will impact packaging presentation.

In-store research is very valuable at the outset of design efforts to understand shopper behavior and retail realities.

Using Research to Inform, Pre-Test & Validate

There are also some clear implications for using shopper research effectively:

- There's an obvious need for consistent shopper and store understanding at the outset of design efforts. At a minimum, there should be consistent process for "going to the store" and gathering a set of key inputs related to shopper behavior, retail and competitive context and the role of in-store merchandising across primary retail channels.

- Finally, marketers must ensure that new packaging systems are working in the larger store context. When actual in-store testing isn't feasible, we're using new tools to assess packaging systems in the full aisle context, including SRP, end-cap displays, and in-aisle signage. For example, in a recent virtual study in the lighting category, we were able to simulate several different scenarios (new packaging only, new packaging with new shelving and signage, etc.), and measure impact on purchase patterns and aisle shopability. We found that the combination of elements—working together and complementing each other—had stronger impact than a packaging change alone.

By integrating shopper feedback—and incorporating the reality of the store—at both the front-end and back-end of design efforts, marketers can help ensure that they are thinking holistically about in-store shopper marketing. They can gather insights (and evidence) that will help them collaborate effectively with retailers, in developing "win-win" solutions that drive category growth.

And perhaps most importantly, they can increase the likelihood that their packaging and shopper marketing efforts are helping their brands to win at retail.

In the Home & On the Shelf

Gathering Insights to Promote New Product Success

New products are the cornerstone of nearly every company's growth strategy and they are a source of major investments in development, research and advertising. However, it's clear that new items face enormous challenges. In fact, new product failure rates are consistently over 80 percent and true "success stories" are rare, as fewer than 5 percent have $50 million or more in first year sales.

Given these long odds, marketers are well-advised to look closely at their processes for new product development, screening, and introduction. And the best place to start is the consumer, who is inevitably the ultimate arbiter of success.

Many new products fail because they get lost in the clutter of the shelf context.

Sourcing Ideas in the Home: The Power of Observation

Where do good ideas come from?

Obviously, there is no single answer to this question. But in our experience across countries and product categories, one commonality is that the most powerful ideas come from consumers. Specifically, they tend to come from *observing* people, as opposed to directly asking them for ideas or solutions.

Indeed, many successful innovations are rooted in a detailed understanding of a product's "life cycle" with the consumer, from purchase through transport, usage, storage and disposal. By tracking this life cycle and exploring underlying "pain points," marketers have developed innovations such as Swiffer—which addressed the limitations and frustrations of home cleaning, and 100 Calorie Packs—which provided the benefits of both portability and portion control.

The 100 Calorie Pack example is particularly instructive, as it reminds us that many successful innovations are not driven by "break-through" technology: Instead, they use packaging innovation (i.e., new delivery systems) to provide benefits, break down barriers to use, and extend products into new usage situations.

For marketers and researchers, the good news is that the internet (and its accompanying shift in cultural norms) has made it easier than ever to connect more closely with consumers. Previously, ethnography studies involved spending days in people's homes watching them make breakfast or do the laundry, a time-consuming (and often tedious) task. Today, we have "digital ethnography" (via webcams, handheld devices and more), with people willing (and often eager) to take us into their kitchens, bathrooms, and bedrooms, sharing opinions and the most intimate details of their lives. And when we do uncover frustrations (both spoken and unspoken), we have new tools (such as online communities and expert panels) that allow us to probe them immediately.

But while these technologies allow us to observe and connect with people more quickly and deeply than ever before, a word of caution is also in order: Like any tools, they can be misused. Thus, it is important to:

Packaging innovation provided a consumer benefit (portion control) and drove incremental product consumption.

- Remember that consumers are generally better at discussing their frustrations and critiquing concepts, as opposed to "solving the problem" for you.

    While "crowdsourcing" (i.e., challenging a group of people with a problem and gathering a wide range of ideas) can be valuable, it can also be important to "give people something to react to."

- Remember that online communities and user panels are often a very engaged and self-selected audience, which is ***not*** representative.

    Therefore, there's a need to clearly separate idea generation (with these audiences) from the screening and evaluation process (with a more representative population).

Testing Ideas on the Shelf: The Importance of Context

Why do many good ideas never translate to successful new products?

Of course, there are many answers to this question as well. However, our research does clearly point to a consistent pattern:

Many promising new product concepts "break down" at the shelf.

They may be rooted in solid propositions—and perform quite well in focus groups and concept tests—yet:

- They are never seen or actively considered by shoppers in store; or

- They fail to convey their proposition (and differentiate from competition) in the few seconds that shoppers spend with them in store.

    In fact, in recent joint research with BASES, we quantified that in-store visibility has enormous impact on new product success.

Our experience suggests that these inter-related problems are rooted in a fundamental dis-connect between marketers and shoppers:

- Marketers develop new products from the "inside-out." They start with a concept, which is painstakingly developed and refined through product testing. Once the formula is finalized and approved, it is raced to market, with packaging and retail presentation often done at the last moment, to meet a launch deadline.

- Shoppers encounter new products from the "outside-in." They first see (or miss!) a new product within a cluttered shelf, in the midst of more familiar alternatives. If the packaging captures their initial attention, they typically spend only 5 seconds "giving it a chance" to differentiate and persuade. In this initial encounter, the package truly is the product, i.e., the product's representation and spokesman.

New product testing often misses this dynamic, by showing new concepts in isolation (without competitive context), relying on concept statements (with far more information than packaging or POS can provide), and allowing for extended exposure (far more time than shoppers would spend in store). As a result, it often overestimates the likelihood of new product success. To avoid this common mis-step, marketers should:

- Screen new ideas within competitive context, as they will appear to shoppers.

     At PRS, we've been using our PRS Retail Lab to place new concepts on shelf and quickly gauge their levels of visibility and pick-up.

- Pre-test new products from the shelf to the home.

     The most valuable new product studies replicate the consumer's full experience, from shopping in store through home usage. This allows us to see if a new product "clears every hurdle" to trial and re-purchase—or "falls down" on a particular dimension (such as visibility, differentiation, price/value perceptions or product delivery).

Improving Success Rates & ROI

New products are a major growth opportunity, but they also present the single greatest challenge in marketing.

New research tools, such as digital ethnography, crowdsourcing and online communities, offer the potential to observe, understand and connect with consumers more quickly and deeply than ever before. If used correctly, they can identify opportunities for valuable innovations. However, they also must be linked to the right processes for screening and validation, to ensure that strong ideas translate into compelling packaging and retail presentation. Companies that use research wisely will be well-rewarded, with higher success rates and stronger return on their new product investments.

New technology such as digital ethnography help us understand the role of packaging in consumers' lives and identify opportunities for innovation.

Bringing Eye-Tracking to the Store

Applications, Observations & Shopper Insights

Marketers are increasingly recognizing the importance of "winning at retail" and influencing the many purchase decisions made in store. In their race to better understand and impact the shopping experience, most companies have quickly learned that observation is the key to shopper research, as there is often a wide gap between "what shoppers say" and "what shoppers do." Asking questions often drives misleading conclusions; shoppers honestly don't know how and why they made decisions. Given the overwhelming amount of stimuli in-store, their thought processes can't be fully rational. Instead, in-store decisions are largely physiological. They are driven by what shoppers see (and miss) in their trips down the aisle.

Given the overwhelming amount of stimuli in-store, the shopping experience is largely physiological and driven by what shoppers see and recognize.

This reality led Perception Research Services (PRS) to explore bringing its eye-tracking technology, which it pioneered over 35 years ago in central location testing, to actual stores. This new form of eye-tracking

(*PRS Mobile Eye-Tracking*) takes the form of a pair of glasses or a small visor, which creates a videotape of each person's shopping experience (including his or her exact focal point) around the store and in the aisle. Importantly (and uniquely), this system provides accurate readings at all distances, which allows for documentation of both "macro-level" shopping behavior (such as aisle navigation and category viewing patterns) and more "micro-level" actions (such as readership of packaging and POP materials). In this chapter, we'll share highlights from three recent studies using *PRS Mobile Eye-Tracking* in retail stores. We'll summarize specific learning from each study and discuss how these findings link to larger underlying "shopping realities" that PRS has seen across studies, categories, and countries. These examples will highlight the added value that can be gained from eye-tracking.

PRS Mobile Eye-Tracking can create heatmaps to illustrate what people see and miss in the store.

"Grab & Go" Shopping

Our initial case study involved a frequently shopped food category: a grocery aisle that many people shop weekly or bi-weekly, as a staple of their diet.

Not surprisingly, our research across numerous retailers and three channels (grocery, mass, and club stores) revealed a largely consistent pattern: Shoppers were on "auto-pilot" in the aisle. They typically spent under a minute in the aisle, grabbed a single product, and levels of observed comparison shopping were remarkably low (about 5 percent). Unfortunately, levels of incremental or unplanned purchases were similarly low, which limited profitability for both manufacturers and retailers.

While some of these findings were obvious through more traditional forms of observation, the eye-tracking revealed a deeper and highly actionable insight: the fact that shoppers were frequently buying the brand they saw first. In other words, shopping in this aisle was not necessarily a matter of people finding "their brand" and putting it in the cart. Instead, shoppers were selecting the first brand (presumably within a set of "acceptable" brands) that met their primary criteria (flavor, form).

For many years, we've known and preached that retail visibility, "Stopping Power," is a key driver of success. However, this study took that learning further, by suggesting that pre-empting competition, via displays, strategic shelving, and breakthrough packaging is critical, particularly in habitual "grab-and-go" categories. Of course, this study also ties to a more universal shopping reality, the burden of too much choice. As categories continue to expand, shoppers everywhere are overwhelmed at the shelf. With hundreds of choices to consider, they instead tune out and default to the familiar or the first brand seen, to save both time and aggravation. As a result, it becomes ever harder for new products to succeed and for marketers to drive incremental purchases. Indeed, in this particular study, it was telling that we saw the highest degree of unplanned purchases (and comparison shopping) in the club channel, where the category was far less complex (with larger packages and fewer options).

In many FMCG categories, shoppers are on auto-pilot and grab the first acceptable brand that they see.

High-Involvement Purchases

A second study focused on a very different category and shopping experience a consumer electronics product that was purchased infrequently and required more information and a larger investment.

Here, our research across several countries (the U.S., China, and Western Europe) and multiple retail channels focused on a different dynamic: The role of various marketing vehicles and materials along the "path to purchase." As with the earlier example, some findings were quite predictable, most notably the significant role of pre-planning such as internet-based research, publicized discounts, and so forth in influencing or "framing" the shopping trip. However, even in cases of extensive pre-planning, in-store observation confirmed that these shoppers were comparing products and making decisions in the aisle.

In this case, the eye-tracking documented engagement with different vehicles (packaging, product displays, and point-of-sale signage or other materials) within the in-store discrimination process. Specifically, we found that when physical product displays were available—typically in computer superstores—they were nearly always the initial source of attention, and the primary driver of decisions. In these situations, POS displays and packaging were generally relegated to a supporting role (confirming specifications, compatibility, etc.). Meanwhile, in channels without product displays, shoppers typically relied on packaging rather than POS materials to compare products.

In fact, we uncovered that shoppers' engagement with different types of POS varied widely. While some materials—most notably those with unique shapes and appearance—were regularly part of the shopping process, many other forms were consistently ignored and most likely represented a waste of resources. The primary implication—that it is better to limit and focus in-store merchandising efforts (less is more)—was quite clear and consistent with what we've seen in other studies at quick-service restaurants, convenience stores, and other retail channels.

Observing these technology shoppers also illustrated a larger shopping reality, which we call the "Great Disconnect." Across categories, we often find that shoppers come to the shelf thinking in terms of users and usage occasions (*Will this product serve my specific need?*). However, in the aisle they frequently encounter a bewildering range of choices that emphasize product forms, features, benefits, or sub-brands. Point-of-sale materials that help bridge this gap by linking features and benefits to users and usage occasion are often the most successful in closing sale and driving incremental purchases.

In higher involvement categories, shoppers are drawn by product displays and look for information that links products with usage occassions.

Stopping Power and Emotional Connection

A third study also centered on in-store signage and displays, but in the very different context of a popular beverage aisle (in North America and South America). In this heavily merchandised category, the primary objective was to understand which POP materials were consistently seen and which were ignored. In addition, we linked eye-tracking to neuroscience measures, to uncover which efforts drove cognitive engagement and a positive emotional reaction.

In this case, the findings highlighted the critical role of store placement and the fact that the location of merchandising can actually be more important than the creative execution. Without question, the clearest and most dramatic learning was that ceiling-based signage was completely ignored. Across dozens of eye-tracking videos, across countries and multiple stores, we did not see a single shopper look upward to engage with overhead promotional signage. This finding is largely consistent with our experience across studies and retail channels. Shoppers may use ceiling-based materials to guide store navigation, but once they are in the aisle, their focus is straight ahead or slightly downward. Thus, point-of-sale materials at eye-level or arm-level (interspersed with packages) have far more visual impact than materials above the products.

In addition, the study revealed an interesting disconnect between retail visibility and emotional resonance. In fact, several of the ceiling-based signs, which were completely missed by shoppers, were actually among the most emotionally compelling to shoppers when they later saw them upon forced exposure. Conversely, some of the most visible displays were not particularly compelling. The implication—and larger reality—is that

Even compelling offers and creative executions are not impactful unless they are positioned properly within the store.

shoppers aren't consciously choosing what to look at in store. Instead, stopping power and in-store visibility is primarily a function of location or placement and contrast with the surrounding environment, and we shouldn't assume that the most compelling displays will be the most visible ones. Therefore, marketers should think of visibility and content as two separate, but equally important, drivers of in-store success. To drive sales, they need to optimize both creative execution and store placement.

Benefiting from In-Store Eye-Tracking

The case studies above illustrate two primary and proven applications of mobile eye-tracking:

- Understanding in-store shopping behavior, particularly the role of visibility within the path to purchase
- Guiding, assessing, and enhancing point-of-sale merchandising, in terms of both creative execution and in-store positioning

In addition, they highlight a primary benefit of this tool, which is its flexibility for use in nearly all retail environments, across countries, channels, etc. Indeed, we've found it valuable in helping marketers identify opportunities and guide in-store marketing strategy for new or alternative retail channels, such as convenience, club stores, and traditional kiosks in developing markets.

Finally, we've found that *PRS Mobile Eye-Tracking* can add considerable value in both qualitative and quantitative shopper research studies:

- In qualitative studies (with 15–20 shoppers), the shopper video-tapes are a primary output, often illustrating an observed behavior, such as shopper confusion or frustration, in a compelling and visceral manner.

- In quantitative studies (with 75 or more shoppers), the value often lies in documenting visibility of specific displays or POS materials, typically via numerical data.

Across applications, the commonality is that eye-tracking gives marketers a "shoppers' eye" view of the retail world. In doing so, it provides them with a richer and more meaningful understanding of the shopping experience and typically a greater appreciation for the clutter and complexity of the shopping environment.

For specific studies and brands, this level of insight typically leads to more effective execution of shopper marketing campaigns. Across studies and over the long term, this perspective also impacts how companies think about in-store marketing and accelerating the transition towards strategies based on observed shopper behavior—"what shoppers do"—as opposed to what they say.

Focusing on the Two Moments of Truth

Uncovering the Drivers of Success & Disaster

Recently, marketers have become more focused on the power of design and far more aware of the power of packaging to impact sales. However, as companies have acted more aggressively in changing the appearance of their brands, we've also seen several high-profile mistakes, most notably the Tropicana disaster, in which a new packaging system led to double-digit sales declines. This has led some clients to ask if there is a formula for leveraging the power of design while minimizing its risks.

With this issue in mind, our firm, Perception Research Services (PRS), recently reviewed our packaging research database (across thousands of studies) to see what it could teach us about the primary factors driving sales gains. This exercise uncovered several interesting insights, with definite implications for both packaging design and shopper research.

True Wins are Difficult to Come By

First and foremost, our analysis revealed that true wins (i.e., major sales gains from packaging changes) are quite difficult to come by. Across studies, while nearly half of the new (i.e., proposed) packaging systems outperformed current packaging in terms of overall packaging effectiveness (as measured by the PRS Packaging Performance Index), only about 10 percent of new systems drove significantly more shoppers to purchase the brand from shelf.

Thus, while a new packaging system might be more appealing or perhaps stronger than a current one in supporting core brand imagery;

these advantages were not very likely to directly impact shopping patterns and translate into sales. In addition, we found that it is far easier to damage a brand than to grow it via packaging. In fact, it's about twice as likely, as approximately 20 percent of new packaging systems drove declines in purchases from the shelf (as opposed to the 10 percent driving significant sales increases).

Of course, a natural next step was to take a closer look at the major success stories, in order to identify the performance measures and design elements that most highly correlated with success. This uncovered a very intuitive, yet powerful, reality: To significantly drive sales, new packaging systems need to have a powerful impact at one of the two moments of truth, on the shelf or in the home.

Visibility is Single Strongest Driver

Across brands and categories, we confirmed that increases in shelf visibility were the single strongest driver of sales increases. While we've long known that "unseen is unsold," this finding goes a step further: It confirms that if a new design system can drive a higher percentage of shoppers to engage with a brand at shelf, it is highly likely to drive purchase. In fact, through studies conducted in collaboration with Wharton and INSEAD, we've found that reexamination (getting shoppers to take a second look at a brand, as measured via eye-tracking) is an even more powerful predictor of purchase. When shoppers take a second look, they are actually reconsidering a brand (giving it a second chance) and bringing it into their consideration set.

Of course, this leads us one step further, to the question of what creates shelf visibility and leads to a second look. Put simply, the one-word answer is contrast. In other words, visibility is not the result of a shopper's conscious decision (*I want to look at that brand.*), but instead a physiological process, driven by the contrast between a brand and its competitors on shelf. Literally, it is what catches the eye.

So what creates contrast? Our analysis revealed three primary drivers: color blocking, unique shapes or structures, and strong brand identity such as a bold logo or visual. In fact, across brands, cultures and countries, we've seen that revolutionary new packaging structures have a far greater likelihood (than graphics-only changes) to create disruption at the shelf, lead shoppers to take a second look at a brand they previously ignored, and, ultimately, to change their behavior.

Interestingly, we've found that declines are not the inverse or mirror image of successes but they are also driven by on-shelf performance. Rather than shelf visibility, we found that *declines in shopability are the factor most consistently linked to drops in sales.* Specifically, we've seen that when shoppers are confused or frustrated at the shelf, it typically takes one of two forms:

- Brand hesitation (*Is this still my brand?*) or
- Product findability (*Where is my product?*).

One or both of these factors create enough hesitation for shoppers to revert to a safer choice (i.e., a competitive brand) and leave the brand, in some cases permanently.

Designing for Retail Realities

New packaging structures can also be powerful in linking to an important and oft-overlooked aspect of shelf presence: Packaging rarely appears as we'd like it to at retail. Instead, packs are frequently knocked over, facing sideways or backwards, partially obstructed, scrunched up and dented or compromised by poor lighting or careless stocking. These retail realities are often the result of packaging systems or structures that don't translate well to the retail environment.

Consider rounded containers, such as those used for many beverages. They may look great in a conference room (or perhaps when viewed in a focus group) when they face directly forward. In-store, however, these

New package structures can help improve shelf presence and drive sales success.

containers are often turned off-center, which can greatly compromise their shelf impact. Bagged products can also be a challenge because they are likely to sag or get scrunched on the shelf, which can impact quality perceptions or make key copy points unreadable.

When marketers invest in packaging structures that limit retail risks and maximize opportunities, we often see a positive return. For example, the new square jar for Kraft mayonnaise makes it very likely that the front label will face outward on shelf, thus creating a clear competitive advantage.

Finally, we've continually seen that packaging systems can break through clutter on-shelf by more directly speaking to shoppers' underlying priorities and thought processes. In many categories, we find a disconnect at the shelf, between the shopper's mind-set, which is often focused on users and usage occasions (*Who is this product for? When would I use it?*) and packaging communication, which typically emphasizes ingredients, forms, and features (diet, organic, liquid, gel, etc.).

For new products, the opportunity often lies in defying convention and using packaging to speak to an underlying need or a specific usage occasion. One excellent example is Nabisco's 100 Calorie Packs, which quickly built a $100 million brand by using packaging innovation to provide portion control and to extend brands into new usage occasions (school lunches, etc.).

Think Beyond Pack Functionality

When most marketers consider the second moment of truth during product usage, thoughts turn immediately to packaging functionality (opening, dispensing, etc.). However, we've found that there is a danger in defining functionality too narrowly. The reality is that we have come across very few cases of major functional problems with current packaging, such as leakage or breakage, which are creating high levels of dissatisfaction.

Instead, we've found that the challenge is identifying unmet (and often unarticulated) consumer needs, and using them as an opportunity to provide differentiating benefits. One frequent example is resealability, which provides value by retaining product freshness and preventing spoiled food. On a spontaneous basis, consumers don't often complain about packaging that doesn't provide resealability. However, when we observe them in their homes, we see that they often work around the issue, by taking the food out of its original packaging and putting it into alternative home storage containers (such as unbranded jars, sealed bags, plastic containers, etc.).

When Chips Ahoy! identified and acted upon this trend (via the Snack n' Seal feature), it was rewarded with double-digit sales gains. Not surprisingly, we've recently seen this trend extend to other companies and categories, such as Target's Archer Farms cereal packaging.

These examples, and their connection to home storage, also link to the larger opportunity in the home environment. Consistently, we've seen that there is a direct and powerful connection between where products are stored and how often they are consumed. In other words, it's critical to avoid getting "lost in the pantry" and it's very important to have packaging that creates a consistently visible branded presence in the home.

The most obvious example is fridge packs, which drove enormous increases in beverage sales upon their introduction. More recently, Heinz drove a 68 percent increase in consumption of its large 64-ounce ketchup product through a more slender package that provided improved storage flexibility within refrigerators.

Structures that are more visible within the home lead to higher consumption.

A Balancing Act Between Disruption & Continuity

The insights gathered from our study of packaging success stories have clear implications, in terms of guiding both design efforts and investment in packaging innovation.

From a design perspective, the findings point to a very challenging balancing act that must be navigated. To make a difference and drive elusive wins at the shelf, designers need to make significant changes that create visual contrast at the shelf and lead shoppers to take a second look and reconsider the brand.

Smaller changes, which are less striking and not evident from three feet away within a cluttered shelf, are very unlikely to influence purchase patterns. However, to prevent major mistakes, designers also need to avoid creating brand hesitation and confusion at the shelf. They need to provide some visual continuity, in order to reassure shoppers and bring them along, which acts as a counterbalance against the imperative for dramatic change.

How can designers and marketers navigate this challenge? Fortunately, recent experience points toward at least one successful strategy, as embodied by successful design changes by Baked! Lay's and Kraft salad dressing. In each of these cases, dramatic and visceral design changes—in color, visuals, and packaging structure—were balanced with continuity in brand identity (to provide reassurance) and very clear product versioning (to facilitate shopability).

On a larger level, our experience highlights the importance of investing in new packaging structures and delivery systems, which hold far more potential (than graphics alone) to positively impact both moments of truth. While dramatic graphics changes can certainly make a difference at the shelf, there's no question that structural innovation is a more powerful weapon, in terms of driving wins in the store and at home.

Focusing on the Store and the Home

Finally, our experience has powerful implications in terms of packaging research. Overall, it suggests that if researchers are to truly help marketers and designers win through packaging, they need to change their focus in several ways.

First, researchers need to spend more time in the store environment. In addition to discussing packaging with shoppers, researchers need to observe them in the aisles. Packaging research has to incorporate and integrate shopper research, to provide an understanding of decision-making at the shelf—and to identify opportunities to break through clutter via innovation.

In addition, in-store research is needed to systematically uncover retail realities that are limiting sales, by compromising how packaging appears on the shelf. These insights should guide design briefs and investment decisions regarding new packaging structures.

Second, there's a greater need for in-home insights. Specifically, more research needs to be done to document the full life cycle of packaging in the home, from purchase and transport through storage, use and disposal. By understanding how packaging fits within consumers' lives, we can uncover opportunities to increase consumption rates through new usage occasions. Importantly, we can also help to ensure that packaging doesn't get lost in the home.

This research also highlights the importance of testing new packaging systems within a realistic shelf context, in order to gather accurate measurements of both shelf visibility and shopability.

It also illustrates the need to test new innovations (new packaging structures and delivery systems) holistically, starting at the shelf, moving to the shoppers' hands, and eventually to the home environment. This level of rigor, measuring impact on shelf presence and in-home consumption, is needed to fully gauge the ROI from new systems and, ultimately, to give marketers the confidence to invest in innovation.

Researchers who embrace these changes, and move beyond a risk-prevention mentality toward a focus on identifying and quantifying opportunities, will become invaluable partners in helping marketers leverage the power of design and win at these two moments of truth.

Winning the Battle at the Shelf
Competing Effectively against Private Label Brands

Over the past decade, private labels have traveled the long road from neglected stepchildren to central components of many retailers' business strategies.

- As retailers have embraced "own brands" as a driver of profit and shopper loyalty, there's been a stunning transformation in the packaging of these brands.

- Retailers now realize that a private label doesn't need to look cheap in order to convey value, nor does it need to mimic the appearance of national brands to suggest comparable quality.

Across categories, the packaging of leading brands must work harder than ever to justify price premiums against private label competitors

- Leaders such as Target and Safeway have used their Organics lines respectively to abandon knockoff design strategies in favor of more sophisticated, branded approaches that highlight the visual cues associated with well-established national brands— prominent branding, compelling visuals, and even structural innovation.

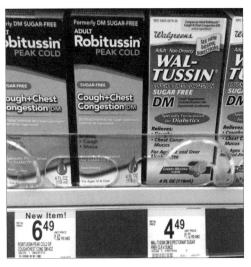

Without question, this revolution in retail branding has placed an increased burden on national brands, which must work harder than ever to justify price premiums. In particular, they've been forced to raise the bar on their packaging to compete at the point of sale against increasingly compelling private label brands. At PRS, we are fortunate to work with many leading CPG companies facing this challenge, in categories ranging from food and beverages to OTC medications and household products. Recently, we reviewed our database and conducted a meta-analysis across studies to see what it would reveal about competing more effectively against retail brands.

Four Guiding Principles

Across categories and brands, several core principles have emerged from our studies that translate into a set of guidelines for packaging brands facing a private label threat.

1. Leverage distinctive visual assets

Certainly, private brands have several built-in advantages in the battle at retail, most notably lower pricing and, increasingly, more favorable shelving. However, national brands also have a major, and perhaps more subtle, factor working in their favor: the power of habit.

Many categories with a strong private label presence are frequent and habitual purchases in which shoppers typically don't invest a great deal of energy. In fact, our in-store studies done with *PRS Mobile Eye-Tracking* have consistently revealed that shoppers are largely on autopilot in these aisles. With low levels of comparison shopping and a high correlation between visibility and purchase, shoppers often buy the first brand that they actively consider. In these cluttered low-engagement categories, people are looking for familiar visual cues (colors, icons, shapes, etc.) to help them "deselect" products and narrow their choices to simplify the shopping experience. The implication for packaging is quite clear: National brands need to build and highlight familiar visual assets (think of Tide's orange hue or Special K's icon), which create visibility and link to brand recognition. By leveraging familiarity—or, if possible, creating "mini-sections"—in the aisle, they can often preempt private label competition, reinforce well-established shopping habits and discourage comparison shopping.

2. Connect emotionally

Shape can be a powerful weapon in facilitating shopping and connecting on an emotional level.

A second, related strategy is for national brands to leverage fully the power of their usage history and advertising budgets in the aisle. To be clear, this doesn't necessarily require linking the packaging directly to the brand's latest promotional campaign. However, it does involve evoking the underlying emotion behind the brand, typically via compelling visuals (the Pampers baby, the Purina pet) that focus on the end user or end benefit rather than the product itself. Alternatively, this approach can involve capturing the essence of the brand through a truly unique design aesthetic (a distinctive voice), familiar icons that convey personality (such as the M&M's characters), or even a particularly compelling on-pack promotion (linked to web-based content, special events, etc.). While the executional strategy may vary, the overriding objective is consistent: to discourage a purely rational decision based on price and quantity by speaking to higher-level motivations, or simply by evoking a smile. The redesign of Kraft Mac & Cheese stands as a successful case in point as it injected personality into the brand and dramatically enhanced its positioning vis-à-vis retail brands.

3. Highlight a point of difference

Beyond the visual and visceral levels, packaging also needs to differentiate and compete at the rational level. Specifically, it needs to give shoppers a reason to spend a bit more as opposed to going with the lower-priced store brand. Here, marketers often misstep in one of two

Kraft redesigned Mac & Cheese to inject personality and differentiate from private label while maintaining its core visual equities.

ways: They rely solely on the power of branding to justify the price premium, or they clutter the packaging with too much messaging, which prevents them from conveying a clear point of difference or superiority. Both strategies are misguided, as across studies:

- We've found that brands highlighting a primary on-pack claim are far stronger in perceived superiority to private label (i.e., worth paying more for), which translates to higher levels of purchase from shelf.

- We've seen that adding extra claims to a pack typically reduces shoppers' visual engagement with the primary claim (as documented by *PRS Eye-Tracking*), which weakens its impact.

While it is difficult to generalize across brands and categories about messaging content, we can say that it's critical to prioritize a lead claim and ensure its visibility. In fact, we've worked with many marketers to develop consistent guidelines for the placement and presentation of on-pack messaging.

4. Add value via packaging innovation

Finally, perhaps the most effective strategy is to change the value equation through packaging structure, functionality or sizing. New pack structures are not only inherently more proprietary and "protectable" than graphics, but also they can make a difference with shoppers on multiple levels—from the shelf through the usage experience—by influencing visibility, imagery, price/value perceptions, usage rates and more. At PRS, we are often asked which innovations really matter to shoppers, i.e., what shoppers will pay more for. Here, the quick answer is that shoppers typically place the greatest value on innovations that link most directly to their value equation:

- By reducing the amount of wasted product (via resealability or full product dispensing)

- By speaking directly to usage occasions (on-the-go packs)

- By offering additional product at the same price
("Get More Free")

Of course, the final point has been discovered by many marketers, which is why we now see large yellow "15% More Free" stickers proliferating in nearly every aisle. However, many companies don't know that there are very consistent ways in which pack sizing impacts price/value perceptions. In joint research with Professor Pierre Chandon of INSEAD, we've uncovered that across categories, shoppers consistently perceive package changes in one dimension (taller or wider) more dramatically than changes in three dimensions (taller, wider and deeper). This has direct implications for maximizing value perceptions, as marketers are well advised to upsize their packaging in one dimension (make it taller or wider)—and to downsize packaging in three dimensions (make it shorter, narrower and thinner in a proportional manner).

Building Private Label into Development & Research

The guiding principles above represent a starting point and framework for thinking about the battle against private label: Is the current packaging working hard enough? How can differentiation be increased? However, to compete effectively on a consistent basis across brands and retail channels, marketers need to incorporate knowledge of private label design strategies into their packaging development and research processes. To that end, we can suggest three best practices.

1. Start with the design brief

A strong brief is the foundation for successful packaging—and at PRS, we've long argued that design briefs should incorporate and illustrate key retail realities such as shelving, lighting and POS that impact how packaging appears to shoppers. Clearly, private label is an important component of this effort: Marketers and designers need to understand

(and ultimately design against) a wide range of store brand competitors, which vary across retailers in appearance, shelving, and POS support. They need to know the strategies of the primary retail competitors: Are they copycats or store brands? Are they brand blocked or interspersed? Do they make directly competitive claims on pack or POS? Does their packaging have functional limitations? While it may not be possible to design for each scenario, this process helps teams to identify the most challenging situations and prioritize efforts accordingly.

2. Incorporate retail brands within packaging development & research

After in-store research has identified several lead competitors, it is important to incorporate these competitors and competitive contexts into the decision-making process. At PRS, we often start by creating digital versions of different retailer planograms. This allows designers to drop in proposed packaging systems and provides a visual reality check through the development process, e.g., *How would this packaging look next to Great Value on the Walmart shelf?* Later, when we conduct on-shelf qualitative and quantitative research with shoppers, we often use two to three different planograms (with varying private label packaging, shelving and POS presence) to gauge visibility, shopability, and purchase patterns. In follow-up attitudinal interviewing (upon direct exposure to packaging), there's often a focus on differentiation from private label, particularly across the core dimensions that link most directly to sales (perceived superiority, price/value perceptions and likelihood of confusion). Importantly, we have shoppers react to the full proposition of packaging and pricing, and then we probe specifically to understand if the packaging is justifying its price premium.

3. Commit to packaging innovation

Finally, given the importance of innovation in competing against private label, it is critical for marketing to commit to exploring new packaging structures, sizes, and delivery systems. This commitment goes beyond increasing the budget for R&D: It also involves developing a shopper research process that measures or quantifies the full value of packaging innovations, particularly in differentiating brands from their private label competitors at the shelf, in hand and in home. It also involves investing in physical package comps for research—to accurately gauge price/value perceptions, particularly when upsizing or downsizing—and ensuring that on-pack claims are clearly highlighting new packaging features and benefits.

Winning at the Shelf

While marketers typically focus their attention on brand building through advertising, promotions and social media, the reality is that their brands will largely succeed (or fail) at the retail shelf, where most purchase decisions are made. At that shelf, they will find far stronger private label competitors than ever before, with more compelling packaging, better

Pack sizing can be a powerful tool in conveying value.

product quality and often a considerable pricing advantage. Without question, retail brands have raised their game and been rewarded with share gains. To win back lost ground, leading CPG manufacturers will need to do the same by acknowledging the challenge, adjusting their competitive mindsets, and developing the right processes to bring more effective packaging to market. Those that do so will be rewarded with packaging that allows their brands to justify price premiums and maintain market share.

Breaking Through the Clutter

Strategies for Success in a World of "Too Much Choice"

It's often said that package design should start with the shopper, but what exactly does that mean? Focus on a specific shopper segment? Highlight a feature that tested well?

We believe that design should focus on the reality of the shopping experience: There are too many choices.

Whether they are in Shanghai, Santiago or San Francisco, shoppers are overwhelmed by 30- and 40-foot product categories, often featuring as many as 200 different choices. From cereal to diapers to motor oil, categories have grown exponentially, fundamentally changing the in-store experience. But what is the impact of "too much choice" on shopping behavior and what are the implications for packaging design?

The overwhelming amount of products on crowded store shelves leads many shoppers to default to their usual product purchase.

What Shoppers Say . . . and Do

Overwhelming choice has transformed shopping from a rational exercise into an emotional one. Shoppers simply don't have the time or "mental bandwidth" to actively and logically compare all of their options. Instead, the experience is driven largely by what shoppers end up seeing in the aisle—and the feelings these packages trigger.

This creates a major challenge for marketers, designers, and researchers. That's because the way shoppers talk about their experiences is often very different from what they actually do in-store. When people are asked about how they shop, they are very likely to speak to logical factors. For instance, if you ask someone how she selected a cold medicine, she might talk about the importance of a trusted brand, the need to treat specific symptoms, and, perhaps, the value of certain safety reassurances.

But when this same shopper comes face to face with stimuli overload in the store, this "decision tree" is often abandoned. In fact, by documenting shopper behavior through in-store eye-tracking technologies, we've uncovered several important dynamics:

Unseen is unsold

Shoppers never see more than two-thirds of products on shelf, which means that many brands aren't purchased because they are never even considered. In categories where there is a constant proliferation of options, shoppers are more likely to buy the first brand they actively consider, rather than compare various brands.

Default to the familiar

People often default to what they've always purchased; shoppers "tune out" and don't bother investigating new options. In fact, our eye tracking videos reveal that most shopping time is spent "searching" for a specific product, as opposed to browsing, comparing products or price checking.

Strong color blocks can help brands to break through clutter and create signposts in the aisle.

Shopping by feel

The overabundance of choice leads people to shop largely by symbols and intuition, as opposed to words and logic. Shoppers use

colors, shapes and icons to navigate vast product categories and to recognize and sort their options. A certain color may signal a specific brand (e.g., green = Fructis), while a shape may intuitively speak to a product form (e.g., upside down = conditioner). These shapes and symbols can also connect on a deeper level. A compelling or familiar graphic, such as the Gerber baby, may provide comfort and reassurance, perhaps by linking to past experience.

Designing for the Shopper

Because of these shopping dynamics, it is essential to use design to break through the clutter and simplify the shopping experience. In our experience, this translates into several guiding principles for packaging development:

1. Design for visibility

The first and most obvious implication of "too many choices" is to design to break through the clutter. The connection between visibility and purchase levels is strongest for smaller brands with limited shelving. Therefore, these brands (such as Wrigley's 5 gum), need to create contrast at the shelf, often by "owning" a disruptive color or shape.

For larger brands (such as Colgate or Pampers), this involves creating a "signpost" in what might be a 40-foot-long aisle to preempt competition and guide shoppers to their specific four-to-six-foot sub-section. In this case, designers need to think about how packaging appears coming down the aisle—and how it can create disruption and impact the selection process from 20 feet away.

Regardless of brand size, the bottom line is that you can't design to the lowest common denominator, to simply "fit in" with a category. Instead, brands need to think of contrast and disruption—and then find ways to provide shoppers with information and to create brand reassurance.

Packages that speak directly to usage occasions, like this Cheerios toddler pack, are intuitive for overwhelmed shoppers.

2. Design for shopability

There is often a disconnect between shoppers' priorities and the way products are organized and named. Although shoppers typically approach the shelf focused on usage occasion, marketers often organize products by features, benefits and sub-brands.

Therefore, we need to create brand architectures that are more aligned with shoppers' thought processes. For example, products and packaging innovations that speak directly to

usage occasions (such as Cheerios toddlers' packs) are far more intuitive for shoppers and far more likely to be successful.

On the design level, it's important to understand the role of shapes, colors and graphics within specific categories. For example, green tends to signal mint flavor in the gum category, menthol in the cigarette category and healthy options in food categories. To facilitate shopping in crowded retail environments, it's best to leverage these category cues, rather than fight them and risk confusion. In fact, packaging changes that confuse shoppers at the shelf (such as the infamous Tropicana redesign of 2009) are the surest route to sales declines.

Large brands also need to strike the right balance between product differentiation and brand continuity across variants. While it's important to visually differentiate new products from the existing line, shoppers often have difficulty comparing packages that are seemingly too different from one another. Shoppers should be able to pick up two variants, look in the same place on the packaging—and quickly understand the differences between them.

3. Connect emotionally

It's also more important than ever for brands to connect on an emotional level. Because shoppers face too many choices to sort through them rationally, packaging needs to do more than speak to the intellect. It needs to look and feel more effective, more fun or, perhaps, more feminine than the competition—and to embody the brand's core positioning in a glance.

Of course, there's no simple formula for this; objectives and strategies will vary by brand. However, packaging structures can be very powerful in differentiating and signaling core benefits. For example, Caress Nutriserum's new packaging uses its shape to embody innovation and femininity, which has translated to in-market success.

Starting at the Shelf

The overabundance of retail choices also has major implications for how we develop, screen and assess new packaging concepts.

First and foremost, it means that we can't rely solely on direct questioning to understand shopper behavior. Instead, we need to begin by observing how shoppers react to packaging and rely on a variety of tools to better understand the "why" behind their reactions.

We also need to improve understanding of the subconscious processes that shoppers use to sort through vast product categories, and to identify and connect with brands. This requires greater investment in "upfront" research to discern the meaning of colors, shapes and symbols within different product categories. It also means uncovering the power of different brand symbols and identifying which design elements drive engagement and emotional connection. In these efforts, the combination of eye-tracking and neuroscience holds considerable promise.

Finally, we must develop, screen and assess packaging options on shelf. Of course, most leading brand marketers have recognized this point (and the limitations of focus groups and web-based surveys), and they have built "the shelf" into packaging validation research.

However, to increase the odds of validation and in-market success, we need to integrate the shelf throughout the design process: We need to begin with store visits to uncover "retail realities," to view new concepts in context—and include the shelf in design screening.

Winning in a World of Too Much Choice

Going forward, as products proliferate and categories expand even further, the brands that win in-store will be those that visually dominate and thwart competition; simplify the shopping experience; and emotionally connect with shoppers and consumers.

To accomplish this, many companies will need to shift how they think about shoppers, research and design. They will need to reduce their reliance on shopper feedback and, instead, rely more heavily on behavioral or observational research that tracks what they actually do.

Brands will also need to approach the design process differently, changing which product factors or dimensions are emphasized and altering how decisions are made. In a more competitive and cluttered world, the companies that embrace these changes—and invest in winning at the first moment of truth—will reap the rewards.

8

Improving the Screening Process
Avoiding Missteps & Identifying the Strongest New Concepts

At PRS, we are fortunate to partner with many leading CPG companies on packaging validation. If there's one question that we are asked most frequently, it is some variation of the following: "How can we increase the likelihood that new packaging systems meet action standards and are recommended for introduction?" This is the right question for marketers, designers, and researchers to ask themselves, because higher success rates reflect a better use of resources on redesign efforts that lead to better packaging on shelf.

There are many potential answers, but without question, effective screening processes are critical to driving success. Companies need to ensure that they consistently identify the most promising new design directions and ultimately bring the strongest options into validation testing. In our experience, it's here that teams often fall into common patterns that lead to the wrong decisions.

Direct side-by-side comparisons of packaging options can be misleading, as they tend to force preferences and overstate differences among options.

How Screening Can Mislead

How can screening research lead teams astray? We've seen several recurring issues:

1. Overstating differences

The most frequent problem is one of magnitude. It's rare that screening research will identify a new package that it is later completely rejected by shoppers in a subsequent study. But it is far too common for teams to walk away from qualitative research believing they have a major win, only to later find out that a new package does little to move the needle versus its competition.

2. Missing problems at the shelf

Screening research often identifies new concepts that are quite strong aesthetically or functionally but are later found to be visually recessive on shelf—or worse, create shopper confusion—both of which typically lead directly to sales declines.

3. Failing to convey the proposition

For new products, screening often brings us packaging concepts that are compelling upon consideration, yet they fail to quickly and clearly convey their proposition and differentiate from competition upon first view.

4. Understating price/value concerns

For new shapes, sizes, and structures, screening can occasionally miss or understate price/value concerns, which are often top-of-mind for shoppers as they encounter new packaging systems.

Why Research Can Mislead

These issues or limitations are rooted in several factors common to screening research whether it takes the form of qualitative focus groups or quantitative web-based surveys:

1. The absence of shelf context

While pack-screening research frequently includes competition, it rarely takes place within shelf context. Thus, it is not surprising that on-shelf concerns tied to visibility and shopability are often missed or understated. The absence of shelf context makes it difficult to gauge whether proposed changes are significant enough to make a difference from three feet away, which is often critical to driving sales.

2. The reliance on comparative questioning

Whether qualitative or web-based, pack screening research frequently centers upon direct comparisons of different options. While comparisons can often reveal insights about specific design elements, they can also be quite misleading. By presenting a scenario that shoppers would never encounter in store (seeing many different packs for the same brand), comparisons take people out of a shopping mindset. As a result, shoppers tend to focus on what they like and "art-direct" along these lines (*Make the logo bigger. Use that shade of green.*). And while this feedback may be honest and well-intentioned, it has a very limited connection to their in-store shopping behaviors.

By forcing preferences and winners, another problem can come up: Comparisons lead shoppers to overstate differences among options. Comparisons may often generate impressive statistics (*Seventy-six percent of shoppers favor Design B over the current package.*). However, they don't give us an accurate sense if a new design system would truly make a difference in terms of brand imagery or shopping behavior if it replaced the current pack on shelf. Thus, they tend to force winners when the reality may be that no design systems truly meet objectives.

3. The shortcuts on stimuli

Often, screening studies take place with renderings, 2D visuals, or virtual stimuli, because clients are not yet able to commit the resources for physical package comps. In some cases, such as proposed changes in graphics or on-pack messaging, this may be perfectly acceptable. But it becomes problematic when screening new pack structures, techniques such as embossing or foils, or added-value features which are more likely to impact functionality and price/value perceptions. If there is one truism of packaging research, it is that the research is only as good as the stimuli.

Improving the Screening Process

Given the wide range of issues that marketers face at the screening stage, there's no way that a single methodology can address all situa-

PRS Retail Labs allow for on-shelf screening of new product and packaging concepts.

tions. For example, we may use a qualitative-quantitative approach to gather feedback on 20 to 25 different pack structures, while a web-based quantitative survey may be more appropriate for identifying the strongest of four to five different on-pack claims. While in-depth interviews (IDIs) are often optimal later in the design process, a triad or mini-group context may be more effective earlier to gather feedback on a wider range of concepts. But across these different circumstances, it is valuable to keep the following guiding principle in mind for screening research: The better aligned that screening and validation research are, in terms of stimuli, methodology, and key metrics, the more likely that their findings will align.

In other words, if the intent is for winning designs from screening studies to also succeed in validation, we should start by pursuing greater consistency between the studies. To the extent possible, we should be asking shoppers the same questions and focusing on the same core criteria, by:

1. Starting at the shelf

Shoppers should first encounter new packaging systems within shelf context, as they do in validation studies (and in store). This simple best practice accomplishes many things at once, as it:

- Grounds people in the shopping context, and thus promotes the appropriate mindset for reacting to new packaging.

- Provides immediate perspective, in terms of whether packaging options are noticeably different.

- Helps ensure a discussion of important on-shelf criteria that link to in-market sales performance (visibility and shopability).

And while some issues, such as shelf visibility, can't be accurately measured on a qualitative basis (or a computer screen), shelf presence should be explored throughout the pack development and screening process.

2. Focusing on the first few seconds

We all know that packaging has a very limited window—often five seconds or less—to make a visceral connection and convey its branding, proposition, and point-of-difference. Thus, screening research needs to address and emphasize immediate communication rather than allowing shoppers to overanalyze packaging options. While extended probes (to understand the "why" behind reactions) have diagnostic value, it is important to begin with a clean read on shoppers' comprehension of, and reactions to, new concepts.

Instilling a shopping mindset and showing new concepts within shelf context reduces people's tendency to "art-direct."

3. Establishing clear success criteria

Often, the underlying objectives of a design effort can get lost at the screening stage, in the midst of hearing what shoppers like. Thus, it is important to remain grounded in the design brief and establish clear criteria for selecting concepts to bring into validation. In other words, it is often more important to identify (and refine) the design that best conveys a certain message or image, as opposed to the one that consumers find most pleasing. And across studies,

marketers and researchers need to change their mindset from identifying concepts that people like towards uncovering those likely to make a difference in store or home.

4. Avoiding the wrong questions

Marketers also need to resist the temptation to ask questions that are likely to generate misleading responses, such as:

- Would you pay more for this feature or benefit?
- Would you be likely to notice this package on shelf?
- Do you find this package confusing?

If asked, shoppers will dutifully, and sometimes eagerly, respond to these questions, to the best of their abilities. But these are issues best addressed by observing shoppers' actual behavior at the shelf: what they see or miss, what they pick up, and what they purchase.

5. "Listening but not believing"

Finally, to paraphrase Mauro Porcini, PepsiCo's chief design officer, we need to listen to shoppers but not necessarily believe them. Consumer input should not be taken literally at face value but rather interpreted and balanced with creativity and strategy. It should influence but not mandate design decisions. This is particularly critical at the screening stage, when a primary objective is to uncover the underlying drivers of why certain pack elements or messages resonate with shoppers—and to apply this insight to further enhance packaging.

At PRS, we've long-applied these core principles to screening research by incorporating shelf presence when possible—and complementing traditional qualitative and quantitative methods with eye tracking. Today, we're taking this a step further via the recent opening of the PRS Retail Lab. This facility includes both physical store aisles and virtual capabilities to allow for on-shelf screening of new concepts, even when physical prototypes are not yet available. In addition, *PRS Mobile Eye-Tracking* allows us to document exactly how shoppers first engage with product categories and packages, to uncover differentiation on shelf and initial communication. At the Retail Lab, we are using many of the same tools and metrics from validation studies at the screening stage. And simply put, the approach is working, as we've documented a significant increase in success rates.

Driving Success

It's important to note that success is dependent on having both a strong screening process and the right set of concepts. With that thought in mind, we can share several guidelines based on our experience across categories.

1. Bring a strong range of options to screening

Too often, we find that clients narrow their scope of exploration prematurely based upon their own comfort level or feedback from senior management. Or, they rush to gather numbers early in the process before concepts have been fully developed and optimized, which also leads towards safer and more evolutionary changes.

As a result, teams end up testing several variations on the same theme or "talking to themselves" with changes that aren't noticeable or meaningful to the shopper. Thus, as a rule of thumb, we recommend including a range of fundamentally different directions at the screening stage with the objective of identifying two to three finalist concepts for validation. It is better to go too far and learn from it than to never push the limits.

2. Link design with messaging

Without question, a compelling new design can positively impact appeal, personality, and brand imagery, just as a new feature can provide a meaningful functional benefit. But to make a difference at shelf and drive purchase, marketers need to consistently link these graphic and structural innovations with strong on-pack messages highlighting the benefit and conveying news. A new appearance may drive a second look from non-users, but it will rarely close sales on its own. Similarly, an on-pack message may be needed to reassure current users and mitigate risk. Therefore, marketers need to ensure that design and messaging are being developed and screened in parallel.

3. Invest in structural innovation

Across brands, categories and countries, we've repeatedly seen that new packaging structures are more likely to impact purchase patterns than graphic design changes alone. That's because new structures can have a dramatic impact across many key performance dimensions: shelf presence, brand imagery, price and value perceptions, functionality, and usage frequency. Although new structures do typically require a larger investment, they are also a high-return proposition.

By employing these best practices throughout the packaging development process and changing their mindset and methodology at the screening stage, marketers can consistently bring stronger packaging concepts into validation—and ultimately drive more wins in both testing and in market.

Getting the Message Right
Insights for Effective On-Pack Messaging

At Perception Research Services (PRS), we are fortunate to assess hundreds of new packaging systems each year, for both new products and re-stages of existing brands. While many succeed, both in validation studies and in-market, we also encounter many new packaging features and graphics that fail to make a difference. Often, this is due to a lack of effective on-pack messaging:

- A new appearance may drive a second look or convey an updated personality, but it is usually not enough to convince competitive users to switch brands.

- A new feature or benefit may be compelling, but it fails to convert new buyers, because so few shoppers even see it upon their first glance at the packaging.

With this thought in mind, this chapter shares our collective experience and perspective regarding both the content and presentation of on-pack messaging, along with several recommended best practices for promoting effective communication.

The bright yellow color (used on many violators) can have negative associations (tied to low quality).

Finding a Compelling Message

There are two primary components to effective messaging, which are arguably of equal importance:

Content – identifying a compelling claim or message, and
Presentation – ensuring that this content is consistently seen.

Of course, it is more difficult to generalize about the former, as the "right message" will inevitably vary across brands and marketing objectives. However, we can share several fundamental principles to guide the development process.

One important role of on-pack messaging is to define or "frame" packaging changes in a positive way.

On-pack messaging is vital in providing reassurance, particularly when shoppers encounter a new look or structure.

1. "Frame" the Packaging Change

When shoppers encounter a new look for a familiar brand, their natural first reaction is to ask themselves what has changed?" Thus, it is vital for the packaging to answer this question quickly and clearly in a positive manner, especially when the brand has a good story to tell—"Improved Formula," for example.

2. Provide Reassurance

It's also important to recognize that shoppers are both risk-averse and increasingly cynical about packaging changes, due to pack reduction/downsizing efforts. So when they see a new package, particularly a new structure or delivery system, some are immediately worried about "making a mistake" (that they are buying the wrong product), while others assume they will get less product or pay a higher price. Thus, one important role of on-pack messaging is to provide immediate reassurance on both product or quantity—"Same great product. Still 12 ounces."

3. Go Beyond "New"

We are often ask us if there is value in putting "New!" violators on the packaging of new products—and the quick answer is yes. However, our experience also suggests that marketers are best served by going a step further and directly linking this message with a phrase that defines the new product's point-of-difference or reason-to-believe, for example: "New. The Fastest Relief Ever."

4. Emphasize Value

Finally, there's no question that at the point-of-purchase, shoppers are often focused on the price/value equation, particularly as they increasingly compare national brands to lower-priced private label options. Given this reality, the best strategy is often to provide an on-pack added value claim, to help justify a more expensive purchase. Across studies, we've consistently found that getting additional product is compelling—and more specific and numerical claims are stronger than more general ones. Therefore, it isn't surprising that a trip down almost any grocery, mass or drug aisle reveals many packs with "15% more free" violators.

When marketers invest in packaging innovation, use of strong on-pack messaging is critical to ensure that shoppers become aware of the new feature or benefit.

Drawing the Shopper's Attention

No matter how compelling, a claim can't be effective unless it is seen—and our experience strongly suggests that shoppers' attention can't be taken for granted. In fact, when we use *PRS Eye-Tracking* to document how shoppers view packages, we often find major differences in visibility and readership levels, based on the location, size, and creative execution of on-pack claims. Fortunately, however, eye-tracking has also revealed universal "best practices" for helping ensure that primary messages are consistently seen.

1. Prioritize a Lead Claim

First and foremost, we know that shoppers don't fully consider packages. In fact, they typically spend under 5 seconds with a fast-moving consumer

goods (FMCG) package and actively engage with only 4 design elements—
perhaps the brand mark, the product name, a main visual—and one message. Importantly, we've seen that adding messages doesn't generally lead
to increased viewing time. Instead, it results in more elements fighting each
other for the shopper's limited attention. Therefore, "less is more" in terms
of on-pack messaging, both in terms of number of claims and the number
of words in a claim. Indeed, we've consistently found that shorter claims,
with fewer words and often larger font styles, are far more likely to be read
than longer ones.

2. Integrate with the Brand Mark or Main Visual

Eye-tracking also shows us that packages are not read like books, in a
pre-defined flow from top to bottom and left to right. Instead, the layout
and design of a package determines how it is first viewed. Shoppers are
drawn to the strongest visual element, usually the brand mark or main
visual, which is often positioned centrally. For this reason, we've found that
violators in the top left or right corners often fall outside the shoppers'
primary viewing flow—and thus are usually missed by about two-thirds
of shoppers (only 35 percent visibility). By contrast, more centrally located
claims integrated with main visuals or brand marks typically have visibility
levels of 50 to 60 percent.

3. Communicate Visually

Of course, creative execution does affect the visibility of on-pack claims.
We've seen the exact same message draw widely varying levels of attention, depending on its treatment—graphic execution, size, positioning,
font style, etc. Predictably, bigger/bolder messaging creates more contrast
and drives higher levels of attention. In addition, we've seen that claims
with visual icons are more likely to be seen than those with text alone.
Thus, when executing multi-lingual packaging, we encourage clients to
communicate key information visually when possible, as opposed to
repeating copy points in multiple languages.

However, based on experience, we'd also caution marketers against going too far in the pursuit of claims readership. For example, across several categories and countries, we've found that bright yellow, which is now the "color of choice" for many violators, carries a negative association—cheap or poor quality—which can detract from brand imagery and product perceptions.

4. "Commit" to Promotional Packaging

Finally, we've seen that promotional endorsements on packages (Olympic logos, linkages to cartoon characters, co-branded ingredients, etc.) often have very low visibility levels—typically under 20 percent—and impact, due to their recessive treatment. However, when executed correctly, we've also seen that cause-related messaging or promotions, such as linkages to charities, can have a very positive influence on brand perceptions and purchase. Instead of "buryng" a potentially compelling story, marketers are often better-served fully committing to it, with dedicated promotional packs that complement the traditional packaging—the Disney pack, the Olympics pack, the Charity pack, etc.

Ensuring Effective On-Pack Messaging

What can marketers do to help ensure effective packaging claims, across brands and initiatives? Here are three recommended "best practices" that can be built into consistent design and research processes:

Develop consistent guidelines for on-pack messaging

As outlined above, there are largely-universal principles to increase the likelihood that shoppers will see claims as they first view packaging. By establishing principles (regarding the size, location and length of violators, for example), marketers can avoid "re-inventing the wheel" or relying on judgment for each initiative. This will help ensure that on-pack claims cross the first hurdle of gaining attention.

Screen alternative claims within a packaging or POS context

Of course, most companies have processes for screening and selecting product claims. However, these studies are typically conducted without packaging or shelf context: Claims are shown in isolation, rather than as they will actually appear to shoppers. Thus, this approach doesn't provide a sense of how well claims work or "fit" with the packaging—in defining a pack change, providing reassurance, conveying a new product's point-of-difference, etc. Even more importantly, testing claims in isolation can provide misleading findings: In the absence of context, consumers tend to say that "more is better." If additional claims or extra words serve to more fully explain a feature or convey an additional product benefits), they will often lead to higher ratings. However, in the real world of cluttered packages, we know that shorter and bolder claims are more visible and impactful. At PRS, we've been working with several clients to screen alternative on-pack claims (content, placement and creative execution), via combination of eye-tracking (to gauge visibility) and interviewing (to assess communication). Ideally, this is done in conjunction with the development and screening of new graphic designs and pack structures, to provide efficiencies and ensure that design and messaging are working effectively together.

Validate new packaging systems with on-pack claims

Across clients, we've encountered varying perspectives as to whether or not new design systems should be assessed with claims and violators. In fact, some companies prefer to test new packaging systems "clean" (without violators), on the premise that claims will change repeatedly over the lifespan of a given pack design. We feel differently, as our experience suggests that the right claim can make an enormous difference in shopper perceptions. Moreover, we've seen that the first few purchase cycles are the most critical, for both new product introductions and re-stages of established brands. Thus, our philosophy is to test packaging as it will first appear on shelf—and to encourage clients to invest the time and energy needed to ensure that they "get the message right" along with the design

As these best practices illustrate, the larger point is that marketers and designers should embrace on-pack messaging as an important and necessary component of effective packaging, rather than an afterthought or a "violation" of their designs. To this end, they need to build claims development and execution into the design process, to help ensure that on-pack messaging is working to complement a new appearance. Those who adopt an integrated approach are likely to be rewarded with higher success rates—and better returns from their packaging investments.

Investing in Success

5 Best Practices for Effective Packaging Research

An important best practice is to develop, screen and validate new packaging within a shelf context.

How can we get better at packaging? This is an increasingly common question, as senior marketers recognize the power of the containers that envelop their products. It's also a question with many valid answers, as there are several potential paths to improvement, including finding the right design partners, investing in innovation, and elevating design within the organization.

However, it is clear that effective packaging research is a critical part of the equation. The right information and insights not only prevent major mistakes, they can (and should) also focus resources and improve return-on-investment (ROI) from packaging innovation and redesign. With that thought in mind, this chapter shares several best practices for using research to improve packaging at an organizational level, across brands, categories, and countries. It also cites examples of how leading companies are creating competitive advantage through packaging research.

Best Practice #1: Validating

The road to better packaging actually starts at the end, with the research that is done just before formal go-ahead decisions. This final step, often termed validation or qualification, is realistically when the most research takes place, and it's the point in the process where companies are most likely to drive consistency in methodology, in sampling and in decision criteria.

And consistency is indeed a primary consideration. If a company applies the same core methodologies and metrics across studies, the benefits go well beyond the ability to build robust databases and norms. Even more importantly, marketers, designers, and researchers can begin to build a common language around packaging. When they speak of shelf impact, for example, they all know what it means, how it is measured, and what success looks like. Conversely, when a company uses varying methods for different studies or countries, it loses this understanding and the ability to systematically measure and improve on an organizational level.

So which validation process should be used? This is a broad topic and the intent here is not to compare or recommend specific methodologies. However, we can suggest three underlying principles to look for in a global validation system:

- It should center upon quantitative multi-cell monadic studies, which simulate the introduction of new packaging vs. competition, rather than side-by-side comparisons of alternative designs for the same brand.

- It should start at the shelf, with accurate measures of shelf visibility, shopability, and purchase, because these on-shelf measures have been validated to be most predictive of in-market performance.

- It should ensure high-quality stimuli that accurately reflect both the shelf and individual packages because any packaging study is only as valid as the quality of what shoppers see and react to.

While these points may seem intuitive, they have major implications in terms of methodology. For example, our experience suggests that shelf sets need to be at least 75 to 80 percent of actual size to gather valid measures, and that physical packs are needed to accurately assess changes in packaging structure. Thus, to get accurate findings, companies do need to invest in both stimuli and more robust methodologies such as in-person interviewing.

Finally, in terms of packaging validation, there are two important factors that often separate the great companies from the good:

- The first is implementation and follow-through! Many companies have best practices in place but lack a protocol for determining which packaging changes or decisions require full on-shelf validation. Thus, some brands, projects, or even countries cut corners and "avoid the system" to save time or money. The best organizations couple a consistent validation process with a project classification system and enforcement process so the best practices are followed.

- Second, the best companies apply the same rigor and discipline of on-shelf testing to new products, to ensure that they break through shelf clutter, convey point-of-difference, and drive trial. Other companies apply best practices only to re-stages, despite the fact that effective packaging and shelf visibility, in particular is absolutely critical to new product success.

Best Practice #2: Screening

One important best practice is to screen and validate pack changes and new products within a shelf context.

Once companies have a consistent validation process in place, their focus often turns to success rates. For example, what percentage of new designs tested meet action standards? What percent win vs. current packaging? Typically, this figure hovers close to 50 percent, which reflects

that it is indeed difficult to drive wins on-shelf. However, it's definitely possible to improve this success rate by changing the screening process used to determine which designs go into validation studies.

While screening approaches vary widely, the commonality is that they generally rely upon side-by-side comparisons of designs ("beauty contests"), which lead shoppers to overemphasize aesthetics and to overstate differences among options.

As a result, marketing and design teams regularly emerge thinking that they have hit home runs, only to find out too late that their new packaging is not really making a difference at the shelf.

To make screening research more predictive of success, the key is to ensure that it emphasizes the same key metrics as validation studies. Most importantly, this involves incorporating the shelf at the earlier stage, to gauge if a new packaging system is likely to significantly impact visibility or shopability, or if a new product is even noticed within shelf clutter. Often, even 20 to 30 in-depth interviews (using physical or large two-dimensional or virtual shelves) can provide greater insights than hundreds of interviews lacking this context. It's also valuable to get a better sense of the first few seconds of packaging communication, through behavioral approaches such as pack viewing patterns and neuroscience measures. These tools can help make the screening process less aesthetically driven and more successful in identifying approaches that will break through, connect emotionally, and ultimately succeed in the store.

To drive this transformation, several companies have developed global networks of retail learning centers. We've found that "mini-stores" provide an excellent context for qualitative screening studies, as they bring shoppers and new packaging concepts into the aisle. Already, we have seen their impact in helping companies recognize when they are "talking to themselves" (through very incremental design changes) and to test a wider range of design options.

Best Practice #3: Benchmarking

In addition to rethinking screening, another path to success is to invest in the right packaging initiatives, and to set appropriate objectives and action standards. Yet while nearly all companies invest significantly in developing and validating new systems, remarkably few have processes in place for deciding when to make packaging changes, or for determining specific redesign objectives. Instead, re-stages typically come in response to competitive changes or declining sales—or perhaps they are driven by new advertising or a new brand manager. Nearly always, they are rooted in intuition about what needs to be "fixed," which may be misguided. The problem is that the research and insight often comes at the end of the process, after a great deal of time and energy has been spent solving the wrong problem, or even redesigning the wrong brand.

An effective solution lies in consistently assessing or benchmarking current packaging at the outset of redesign efforts, relative to competition and historical norms. This process, which we call package baseline, is primarily a matter of moving the control cell (from an eventual validation study) up in the project timeline, so that the learning can be used to refine design objectives and inform action standards. Often, we also include an additional name-only cell to uncover visual equities (via drawing exercises) and emotional triggers (via neuroscience), and to gauge the contribution of current packaging to brand imagery. (*Are we selling because of—or in spite of—our packaging?*)

A few forward-thinking organizations have actually taken the baseline process a step further, by instituting annual or biannual audits of current packaging vs. competition. These audits help to allocate resources and investments across the company, by uncovering which brands are most in need of packaging changes. They also serve as a starting point for these redesign efforts by identifying areas of competitive disadvantage or weakness, which often translate to specific and focused redesign objectives.

In-home ethnography can identify opportunities and drive innovation.

Best Practice #4: Innovating

Along with preventing mistakes and increasing the likelihood of successful changes, packaging research should also help drive breakthrough innovations.

And the reality is that revolutionary, game-changing new concepts rarely come from studying current or competitive packaging. Instead, they are typically rooted in addressing major barriers or uncovering unmet, and often unarticulated, consumer needs.

To identify these issues and opportunities, it's best to start at the store. Walking the aisles quickly reveals that packaging often doesn't appear as intended, due to the effects of shelving, signage, or merchandising (compromising legibility, obstructing branding, etc.), or the packaging structure itself (bags knocked over, packages not facing forward, stock-outs, etc.). These retail realities serve as barriers to purchase, which directly impact the bottom line. And while these challenges can't be fully eliminated, they can be mitigated through effective graphic design and investment in better packaging structures and merchandising systems. However, for this to happen, there needs to be a consistent process for visiting stores, classifying these issues, and feeding this information to marketing, design, and R&D teams. Several leading companies have recently begun doing these "retail reality-checks" in a disciplined way, as an input to design and innovation briefs. This process helps ensure that packaging investments solve major problems on the shelf.

The home is clearly another valuable source of big ideas. Specifically, by documenting the packaging life cycle, from purchase, through transport, storage, usage, and disposal, companies can often identify opportunities and uncover unmet needs. Often, we find that the biggest wins come from driving increased consumption by making packaging more visible in the home or by tailoring packaging more directly to specific usage occasions. Indeed, some of the most dramatic and profitable breakthroughs have come from simple ideas (such as fridge packs and 100-calorie packs) rooted in in-home ethnography. Thus, a fourth best practice is to develop a consistent process for reaching out to the store and the home as the most likely sources of breakthrough innovation.

Best Practice #5: Integrating

Finally, the best companies recognize that packaging is one part of a larger effort to win at retail. To put it another way, they know that it is difficult to create great packaging without an underlying understanding of the shopper, and of how packaging interacts with shelving, merchandising, and other in-store variables.

To this end, more companies are breaking down the silos within their organizations that separate packaging research and shopper insights. On one level, they are conducting in-store observational research at the outset of redesigns to ensure that the shopper and the retail insights are incorporated within design briefs. At our firm, this has involved taking eye-tracking technology to the store, to document aisle navigation, interaction between packaging and signage and the purchase decision process.

In addition, marketers are increasingly evaluating packaging in a broader context or using packaging studies to assess alternative planograms or point-of-sale merchandising strategies. We have used virtual shopping tools to assess packaging in the aisle and in the context of end caps, shelf talkers, and alternative shelving adjacencies. In some cases, this has allowed us to isolate the added-value and potential ROI from in-store signage. In others, we've found that alternative shelf placements have had an enormous impact on visibility and the purchase or trial of new products.

Thus, on an organizational level, a fifth best practice is to build bridges between packaging and point-of-sale/shopper research, in order to improve packaging, to benefit from cost efficiencies, and to gain a more holistic understanding of how to win at retail.

Packaging Can Make a Difference

As companies recognize the power and importance of packaging, they will also come to realize that it is not easy to systematically get better across brands, business, and regions. However, market research leaders can make a difference by instilling the right processes and ensuring that their organizations consistently:

- Identify primary issues and opportunities, through store-based research and in-home ethnography.

- Know the strengths and limitations of their current packaging, via benchmarking or baseline research.

- Allocate resources toward the right brands and projects, through auditing and cross-study analysis.

- Properly screen and validate new concepts, by focusing upon on-shelf performance.

Companies that incorporate these best practices are likely to dramatically improve their odds of packaging success. They are less likely to divert energy to the wrong efforts and to end up "talking to themselves" with modest packaging changes that don't make a difference on the shelf. Ultimately, the investment in consistent and proactive packaging research processes will pay off in a stronger ROI.

Improving Success Rates & ROI
Avoiding 5 Common Mistakes

Perception Research Services (PRS) has worked with clients over 40 years to help them develop effective packaging and win at retail." And without question, over that time, our belief in the power of packaging has only grown, as we've seen many success stories where innovative packaging has built brands and driven sales.

However, our experience also suggests that many marketers are not fully or consistently leveraging packaging as a marketing vehicle. In fact, across more than 10,000 studies, we've found that only 50 percent of new packaging systems provide a significant improvement in overall performance, relative to current packaging. While an optimist may say, "The glass is half-full," there's clearly room to improve this success rate.

If packaging changes aren't noticeable on-shelf (from several feet away), they're unlikely to impact purchase patterns.

With this thought in mind, we recently reviewed our database of past projects, to identify key drivers of success—and failure. Specifically, our objective was to understand why some initiatives failed to meet expectations and to identify systematic patterns that were limiting success. This chapter shares key themes from this analysis, along with several recommendations for improving the return-on-investment (ROI) of packaging.

Five Common Missteps

Certainly, there's no single explanation as to why some initiatives succeed and others don't meet expectations. However, across brands, categories, and countries, we have discerned five common patterns or actions that are highly correlated with failure, including:

1. Investing in unnecessary redesigns

Most large CPG companies have consistent research systems in place for assessing or "validating" new packaging systems prior to launch. However, very few use consumer-driven processes for determining when to redesign their packaging, or when to invest in added-value packaging systems or features. Instead, most packaging changes are driven by the judgment of a new brand manager, often in reaction to competitive changes, declining market share, or a desire to "create some news." As a result, considerable resources are spent on innovation or redesign efforts that aren't necessary or appropriate. What we've found is that marketers and designers often tire of their brand's packaging well before shoppers do.

2. Solving the wrong problem

A related issue is that many efforts are rooted in misguided assumptions about the brand and its packaging, e.g., "the packaging looks old," or "it needs to be easier to hold." Thus, a great deal of time and energy is channeled in one direction, only to eventually uncover a very different issue by way of on-shelf or in-home testing. For example, "improving shelf visibility" is a standard objective on nearly all design briefs. And while visibility is absolutely critical for smaller brands and new product introductions, shopability and sub-brand differentiation are often more pressing issues for large master brands, such as Colgate, Dove, and Tide.

3. "Walking away" from core design equities

In today's world of overwhelming clutter and choice, purchase decisions are driven primarily by what people see (and miss) and by

Across categories, PRS has found that structural innovations are likely to drive sales gains particularly when they provide clear user benefits and/or link to new usage occassions.

When redesigning familiar brands, it is important to evolve core design equities rather than abandoning them.

how they feel. Thus, visual equities—including unique, ownable shapes, colors, and icons—are more important than ever to help shoppers navigate expanding aisles and identify familiar brands. And not surprisingly, the majority of "disasters," in which packaging changes have led to sales declines, are cases in which new packaging lacked the familiar visual equities and created confusion or hesitation at the shelf, leading consumers to ask questions such as, "Is it still my brand?" "Where's my variety?" or "Have they changed the product inside?" Of course, brands can't stay stagnant, but the key to successful re-stages is properly balancing disruption and continuity: If there's a dramatic change to one core visual equity such as a new package shape or a primary visual, it's typically best to retain other core elements, such as package color and brand identity. For example, when Kraft Mac & Cheese modified its primary graphics to inject more personality and to distance the brand from private-label competitors, they wisely maintained the Kraft branding, the primary blue-and-gold color scheme, and the spoon visual, all of which provided reassurance to shoppers. In addition, marketers should ensure that front-of-pack messaging helps explain or "frame" dramatic changes in packaging appearance, e.g., "New Look," or "Improved Formula."

Before   *After*

4. Not moving the needle

It's perhaps inevitable that a few high-profile disasters grab headlines and imply that all packaging changes are inherently risky. However, we've actually encountered fewer cases of companies going too far with new packaging, and many more cases of new packaging systems that didn't move the needle in terms of perceptions or shopping behavior. Often, it is due to one or more of the following reasons:

- The packaging change isn't noticeable on shelf (from 3 feet away).

- The new look is not linked to a clear message, i.e., a reason to believe or reconsider.

- A new feature or functional benefit, such as resealability, is not highlighted on the package.

This misstep speaks to the importance of linking packaging innovation and graphic design to strong on-pack messaging: A change in appearance may lead a shopper to take a second look at a brand, but a clear and compelling on-pack message is usually needed to win over a new user.

5. Ignoring the retail and home context

We've found that marketers sometimes lose sight of the fact that packaging needs to work in both the store and in the home.

In the store, packaging is subject to the retail realities of shelving, lighting, and merchandising, and often appears in the context of point-of-sale materials (displays, shelf talkers, etc.) or shelf-ready packaging. All of these factors directly affect how shoppers encounter the brand (which panels they see, etc.) and can compromise packaging communication. While it's certainly not possible to design for every retail scenario, these issues can be mitigated by designing for the worst-case scenario and ensuring that packaging and POS are designed to work together.

In the home, we know that storage location and thus in-home visibility can have a significant impact on consumption. Thus, it's important to ensure that packages "fit" within kitchens or bathrooms and look good enough to be displayed, or they risk being lost in the garage or closet. As important, we've consistently found that many of the most successful packaging innovations are those that link directly to new usage occasions, such as on-the-go packs, or to perceived value, for example, resealability to prevent spoilage and waste.

Driving Success, Increasing Packaging ROI

While we've focused largely on what not to do, the encouraging news is that companies can systematically increase their likelihood of success with package design. In fact, across our largest clients, we've found that major variations in success rates are tied largely to differences in packaging development and research processes. Most notably, the most effective companies invest consistently in upfront learning and structural innovation.

Upfront learning

Across nearly all organizations, research is weighted heavily toward back-end validation to inform final decisions. And while this testing is certainly valuable and necessary, the learning that it provides comes at the very end of the process, when investments have already been made—and often when teams are up against deadlines or are committed to making changes. To improve the process, companies need more information and insights at the outset of design initiatives, to identify opportunities, allocate resources appropriately, and provide direction. Specifically, they need to understand the strengths, limitations, and equities of their current packaging.

For many clients, we've established baseline research as a best practice at the start of design initiatives. By evaluating current packaging relative to competition—on-shelf, in-hand, and in-use—and by identifying design equities via drawing and recognition exercises, we are able to inform design briefs and set clear objectives and action standards. Ultimately, this helps ensure that each redesign effort is solving the real problem and addressing an actual shopper need or competitive disadvantage.

A second best practice is to integrate the shopping context and store environment into the design brief, by documenting the shopper's path-to-purchase, the retail realties of key channels, and the role of packaging vis-à-vis POS materials in the shopping experience.

Increasingly, this process includes understanding the digital world, including the interaction between online and brick-and-mortar shopping, and the role of smartphones and QR codes in the aisle. Collectively, this shopper insight helps define the core mission of the packaging and determines how to properly adapt packaging to different retail contexts, such as club and convenience stores. Of course, parallel efforts should also happen in the home, to document the packaging life cycle—from purchase through transport, usage, and disposal—and to understand how packaging fits within consumers' lives. This in-home ethnography nearly always yields rich learning related to value drivers, barriers to usage occasions, and sources of frustration, which are critical in guiding innovation efforts.

Structural innovation

Our years of experience have consistently reinforced the value of structural innovation. Simply put, we've found that new packaging structures are more likely to drive success than graphics-only changes. That's because new shapes, materials, and delivery systems can have a significant positive impact on shelf, in hand, and in the home, and across nearly all key dimensions of packaging performance—shelf visibility, shopability, imagery and emotional connection, value, and usage. In addition, structural packaging innovation will almost surely play a major role in addressing the core issues and transformative challenges shaping our world, including globalization, public health, and sustainability.

Thus, as we look ahead, we'd encourage organizations to push the envelope and invest in packaging innovation that is:

- Informed by knowledge of the shopper and store,

- Rooted in an understanding of the brand's packaging objectives and equities,

- Focused on key sources of value, and

- Reinforced via effective on-pack messaging.

Companies that apply this discipline to their efforts—and avoid several common missteps—will be rewarded with higher levels of success and a stronger return from their packaging investments.

Doing Simple Design Well
Leveraging the Power of Clarity & Simplicity

For many years, our studies have demonstrated the power of simplicity in packaging design. Specifically, we've seen that simple packages can help brands:

"Break through shelf clutter"

When other packages are "shouting" through bold colors and large fonts, it is often the simple package that creates contrast and invites shopper consideration.

Embody desirable brand attributes (honest, natural, real, organic, etc.)

"Looking simple" also ties well to other primary marketing trends, such as a "retro" look that hearkens back to simpler times.

Convey key claims and messages

PRS Eye-Tracking studies have shown that shoppers typically "take in" only 3 or 4 elements when first viewing packages. Therefore, adding claims doesn't typically improve communication: It only creates clutter and divides shoppers' limited attention more narrowly.

In recent years, there has been a trend towards simplicity, as marketers aim to embody honesty and clarity through their packaging.

Recently, with the success of method and Apple, simplicity has become a mantra in the design world. Thus, we've seen a wave of minimalist designs featuring generous amounts of white space, black type and basic font styles. Unfortunately, however, our studies suggest that this approach has driven mixed results. While there have been some success stories, we've encountered other cases in which simple designs have been perceived as cheap and generic by shoppers. We've also seen that limited packaging information can create significant confusion and frustration at the shelf. With these potential risks in mind, we'd like to offer several guidelines for "doing simple well."

Think Beyond White!

There's nothing inherently wrong with white packaging, as it certainly works well for Lean Cuisine, Pepperidge Farm, and Band-Aid, among other brands. However, we've seen that there is danger in taking the call for "white space" a bit too literally. White packaging tends to be associated with diet/low-calorie products and private label. If taken too far, it can definitely be polarizing. In fact, we've typically seen that about 10 to 15 percent of shoppers have negative reactions to pre-dominantly white packaging, which they perceive as dull, cheap, generic, etc.

Therefore, it's important to think about the percentage of white on pack—and to balance a white background with the strong use of color or dynamic visuals. Starbucks coffee is one brand that appears to have managed this "balancing act" well, as it retained its white equity, but moved from a more minimalist approach to a new design system that integrates colorful, intriguing visuals tied to different flavors. Renuzit is another brand that appears to have struck an effective balance of white and color, as colorful visuals are used to delineate scent.

While white packaging can help convey simplicity, it can also be polarizing (as some perceive it to be dull or generic).

The bigger message, however, is that simplicity doesn't need to be equated with white. It can involve minimizing copy and highlighting the product—as illustrated by Palmolive Pure and Clear—or simply "cleaning up the package" with fewer, bolder claims. We've found these approaches to be successful in terms of both shelf presence and communication, while avoiding some of the risks associated with white.

Consider the Channel, Category and Brand!

While it's often tempting to replicate Apple's minimalist look, it's also critical to meet shoppers' informational needs in different stores and product categories. For example, in image-driven categories with low information needs, such as spirits, cosmetics, beverages, candy, etc., it may be very appropriate and acceptable to have very simple brand-focused packaging. Simplicity can also work in categories and retail channels (such as technology stores), in which high levels of sales help, merchandising, or product demonstrations supplement the packaging.

Showing the product through the packaging can also be an important cue for simplicity, authenticity and quality.

However, this is generally not the case in more complex categories and across most retail channels (mass, drug, grocery, etc.). When sorting through over 200 SKUs at shelf, shoppers do need key information to help quickly find the right product—and to feel reassured about product delivery. Thus, while the very clean and minimalist Rembrandt packaging stood out on the toothpaste shelf and visually suggested white teeth and product efficacy, it hindered shop-ability and ultimately drove down sales.

Brand-level dynamics should also be considered. Often, very familiar brands and products (like Oreo, M&M's, etc.) have "permission" to focus on imagery and tap into shoppers' existing positive emotions, without the need for excessive claims and copy. However, for new products and smaller brands, there is a need to convey a clear point-of-difference and reason to believe. Simplicity can help a brand "break through clutter" and drive initial attention, but it is not enough to close the sale.

Culture Matters!

Finally, it's important to keep cultural aesthetics in mind, when designing globally or for specific ethnic audiences. Generally speaking, the trend towards minimalism has been driven by Europe—and we've seen that Northern Europeans are the most likely to equate simplicity with sophistication.

Conversely, Asia has traditionally been on the other end of the spectrum. Bigger and louder has typically been perceived as better, while simpler packages have been associated with basic, lower-end products. Similarly, the Latin design aesthetic has traditionally favored stronger, bolder colors, while shoppers in developing markets are often more "information-hungry" and need additional product reassurance.

This does not mean that we should abandon clarity and simplicity as we cross borders or speak to ethnic audiences. However, it does suggest that "simplicity" needs to be adapted appropriately to different regions and audiences through varying use of color, claims, etc.

Simplicity needs to be adapted appropriately to different regions: where some cultures relate simplicity with sophistication, others associate simple packages with lower end products.

A Question of Balance and Prioritization

Overall, PRS' experience still strongly suggests that "less is more" in packaging communication. Indeed, we need only to walk down any grocery aisle to be reminded that the "noise" is overwhelming, and that simpler, more focused packages are more likely to get shoppers' attention and convey key messages.

However, as this chapter illustrates, it's not all that easy to do simple well. Instead, it involves a "balancing act" on several levels:

1. Pursuing simplicity, while avoiding a boring, stark, or cheap appearance.

2. Keeping it clean, while providing shoppers with key product information.

3. Designing globally, while minding cultural preferences and sensitivities.

In addition, and perhaps most importantly, simplicity requires making hard decisions and prioritizing messages. It means resisting the temptation to put "everyone's favorite claim" on the label. To do this well, we need to do the right "homework" before and during the design process to:

- Understand shoppers' decision process and information needs at the shelf.

- Identify a brand's single most powerful and differentiating claim and avoid a "laundry list" approach that clutters packaging and compromises clarity.

- Effectively visualize key features and benefits, and mitigate the need for excessive copy.

- Uncover when they have "crossed the line" from simple to stark.

Marketers and designers that do this homework will be well-positioned to "clean-up" their packaging without sacrificing vital communication—and to arrive at simpler, more impactful packaging that wins at the shelf.

Packaging & In-Market Impact
Optimizing the Rollout of New Packaging Systems

At PRS, we evaluate hundreds of new packaging systems annually and our clients often (and understandably) ask if we are able to accurately predict the impact of packaging on in-market sales. Fortunately, the quick answer is "Yes!" This fact has been validated by "meta-analyses" conducted by clients, analyzing PRS study findings and sales data across more than 50 studies. It has also been illustrated by numerous cases of both "successes projected" and "disasters foretold" for both re-stages and new products. Through these analyses, and academic research conducted at Wharton and INSEAD, we've also been able to define a proven relationship between on-shelf performance measures (purchase from shelf, shelf visibility and shop-ability) and sales in market.

However, the more complex reality is that the connection between "pre-testing" and in-market performance is inexact. The primary reason is clear: In studies, we nearly always isolate packaging as a variable, while holding all other factors constant. But as we all know, the "real world" is rarely this clean. Packaging changes often accompany modifications to other elements of the marketing mix such as advertising and pricing, and they must "live" in an ever-changing retail and competitive context.

With that thought in mind, this chapter takes a closer look at the key factors impacting the in-market performance of new packaging. While these elements are complex and varied across brands, categories, and retail channels, we believe that approaching them systematically can yield insights to optimize packaging roll-outs and increase the likelihood of success.

Identifying the Key Drivers

Certainly, there are myriad issues that can impact how new packaging appears and performs in-store, from competitive activity to the "retail realties" of shelving and lighting. However, in our experience, we've consistently encountered three dynamics that can dramatically impact shopper behavior.

"Soft" rollouts

Over the years, our clients have shared a "rule of thumb" that new packaging often drives a sales decline in its first few months in market, before stabilizing and occasionally driving sales. Typically, this pattern is accepted as inevitable and spoken of in terms of shoppers "getting used to" new packaging, which becomes familiar after 1 or 2 purchase cycles. However, we'd offer an alternative hypothesis: Confusion at shelf driven by "soft" rollouts of new packaging.

Soft roll-outs can create confusion at shelf if shoppers encounter two different packages for the same product.

When new packaging systems are pre-tested, the scenario is nearly always that of a complete and clean roll-out, with a full new design system on shelf. However, a trip to any local grocery or drug store reveals that this is not usually the in-market reality. For pragmatic and financial reasons, companies often allow old packaging to "sell-through" or introduce a new design on "leading" SKUs, as they complete the graphic design for the others.

Unfortunately, this is a recipe for confusion for the shopper (and perhaps the store personnel), who may encounter two packages for the same product or a very fragmented appearance of the brand. The result can be just enough hesitation (*Which is the right one? Is one of them a private label knock-off?*) to lead him or her to a "safer" choice.

It's important to provide on-pack reassurance to help shoppers through this transitional period.

Certainly, the most obvious implication is to invest in full packaging roll-outs when possible. However, this pattern also illustrates the importance and value of providing on-pack reassurance (i.e., "New Look, Same Great Taste!"), to help shoppers through this transitional period. In fact, we've seen some companies go even further to "pre-announce" upcoming packaging changes for major brands, such as Baked! Lay's.

Point-of-sale support

A second factor impacting new packaging performance is in-store support, which can range from end-cap displays to in-aisle signage and shelf talkers. In fact, we've seen several situations in which extensive in-store support appeared to accelerate (or drive) success far beyond what would have been projected from a packaging change alone. That's doubly true for new product introductions, which frequently struggle to overcome their limited number of facings on shelf and absolutely need signage to generate visibility and shopper awareness. U by Kotex and Colgate Optic White stand as two recent examples of new products that were supported heavily and effectively in-store, leading to successful launches. With that said, we've also found that it is dangerous to rely on POS to "save" a poorly designed packaging system. In too many cases, in light of disappointing test results, we've heard clients reassure themselves that they will "fix the problem" through advertising and in-store support.

In-store support can be critical in creating awareness for new brands or packaging designs. However, it is unlikely to "save" a confusing or poorly designed packaging system.

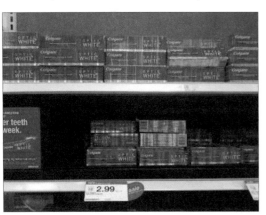

But if the packaging is fundamentally confusing or alienating, even a significant investment is very unlikely to overcome this. In other words, in-store support can make a good packaging system that much more impactful, but it can't make a bad system good.

Perhaps most importantly, marketers need to understand the respective roles of packaging and point-of-sale signage in the shopping experience, within their aisle and across varying retail channels (grocery, club, convenience, etc.). Once they understand this dynamic, often through in-store interviewing with *PRS Mobile Eye-Tracking*, it is a question of ensuring that the two vehicles work together and complement one another. For example, point-of-sale signage is often effective in creating a visceral or emotional connection with shoppers, while packaging is typically stronger at facilitating product selection and conveying key features or benefits.

Changes in pricing or quantity

Packaging changes are often part of larger brand re-stages tied to new advertising or aimed at a more premium positioning or they involve significant investments in new packaging structures, more differentiated packaging, more sustainable packages, etc. For marketers, there's an understandable desire to recoup these investments, often by linking the brand's new appearance to a higher price point or perhaps a reduced product count. However, from a shopper's viewpoint, new packaging represents a signal to switch off "auto-pilot" and re-consider a brand's proposition. Almost inevitably, even a compelling new package raises at least a brief reassessment or instant of uncertainty—*"What's this new look all about?"* Thus, a package change is the moment that shoppers are most likely to notice a pricing or quantity change, and potentially to "define" the pack change in this negative light—*"It's about raising the price and ripping me off."* Sadly, this trend has been accelerated by growing consumer skepticism, linked to experiences in which "sustainable packaging" turned out to be smaller packs and reduced quantity.

The net result is that changing packaging and pricing simultaneously appears to have a multiplier effect, leading to significantly more risk than either change would have incurred individually. And, in today's world, this risk may be amplified further, given shoppers' ability to share their indignation (and influence many others) via the social media. Unfortunately, it is a lesson that many companies have learned the hard way, as compelling packaging re-designs have been undermined by negative reaction to accompanying price increases.

For marketers, the primary "take-away" is to tread very cautiously on pricing changes and perhaps err on the side of waiting several purchase cycles, until shoppers have become familiar with new packaging. Perhaps as importantly, they should also be pro-active in "framing" packaging changes in a positive light, via on-pack and in-store messaging. Kraft Salad Dressing stands as one good example. When introducing more environmentally friendly packaging, the messaging highlighted both the consumer benefit (25% more Free) and the environmental benefit (80% less packaging).

Moving Towards Better Execution, Research & Measurement

The issues outlined above translate into several clear principles for optimizing the roll-out of new packaging systems and increasing their likelihood of in-market success:

1. Investing in clean transitions, so that only new packaging appears on shelf.

2. Investing in point-of-sale support, particularly in terms of driving attention or visibility for new products and smaller brands.

3. Ensuring that on-pack messaging provides necessary reassurances or "defines" the packaging change.

4. Avoiding the temptation to change packaging graphics and pricing (or product count) simultaneously.

In addition, there's certainly an opportunity to use research more effectively, in order to more accurately project (and impact) in-market outcomes.

- On one level, this means pre-testing packaging as it will actually appear to shoppers in store, within a full shelf context and with anticipated pricing and on-pack messaging.

- On a broader level, it requires thinking more holistically: Rather than assessing packaging in isolation, marketers should be thinking in terms of "optimizing point-of-sale presentation" and testing scenarios that incorporate changes in shelving, product assortment, and point-of-sale merchandising.

We are now able to assess new packaging systems in full store and aisle context, including end-caps, in-aisle displays, and on-shelf signage. Importantly, we are able to show this packaging and store context at approximately life size, rather than on a computer monitor, which we've found to be critical to accurately gauging on-shelf performance. In a recent study, *Virtual Aisles* allowed PRS to gauge the impact of a new packaging system—with and without POS support—on sales growth for both the test brand and the full category. The findings helped our client to validate its investment in merchandising.

The final piece of the puzzle is stronger in-market measurement. While nearly all major CPG companies claim to acknowledge the power of packaging, remarkably few have disciplined processes for systematically tracking the impact of pack changes on in-market sales. If post-launch sales tracking can be done consistently and linked to documentation of key factors tied to each change (in-store support, pricing changes, etc.), marketers, designers, and researchers will all benefit greatly.

- Marketers will be able to properly value packaging within their market mix modeling and better understand the key factors driving in-market success within their categories.

- Designers will see greater investment in their field, as companies truly recognize the power of packaging and become more confident in its ability to drive sales.

- Researchers will be able to enhance the predictive power of their studies, based on a consistent feedback loop of sales data.

Over time, this will create a virtuous cycle, as better information and insight leads to more investment and more effective launches of new packaging.

On-pack messaging is particularly important when shoppers encounter new packaging structures such as including more environmentally friendly alternatives.

Brands Without Borders
Strategies for Effective Global Design

In an increasingly connected and competitive world, it's easy to see the logic and appeal of global packaging. There are potential economies of scale in manufacturing, along with obvious marketing efficiencies associated with featuring "one look" from New York to New Delhi. But while the idea of global design can be simple and elegant in theory, it can be quite difficult in practice. Packaging, like so many global marketing decisions, is ultimately a balancing act between global continuity, local customization and, in some cases, between long-term brand strategy and day-to-day execution. Marketers and designers that respect this balance and acknowledge the many local challenges facing global packaging are far more likely to arrive at effective solutions.

A single look or visual image is rarely compelling on a global level because perceptions of beauty and appetite appeal differ widely by country.

Diversity in Formats

Consider, for instance, that packaging needs to work in a wide range of global retail contexts, like the high frequency store, the locally-owned bodegas, kiosks and stalls that serve more than five billion customers globally—80 percent of the world's population. These kiosks are a primary shopping venue in many of the world's largest and fastest-growing economies, including India, China and Latin America, but are often small and dimly lit, with multitudes of products shelved very tightly, which makes for an extremely cluttered and challenging shopping experience.

These retail formats place a heavy premium on very simple and clear packaging. Strong branding and clear variant communication are particularly important, because of the format's "point and retrieve" mode of shopping—shoppers are often across the counter from the products they are buying, with the shopkeeper assisting in the purchase.

What's more, typical high-frequency-store shoppers visit their stores nearly every day, due to irregular income and the need to make small purchases. As such, price considerations are top-of-mind, which means there's an overriding need for packaging to convey or reinforce value.

Of course, packaging structures in high-frequency stores are also quite different from those most common in North America and Europe. Typically, they are much smaller to allow for lower, more accessible price points.

For instance, there's the sachet, which is commonly used for shampoo and laundry products. This smaller pack leaves far less "real estate" than the large bottles or boxes found in our local Walmart or Tesco stores, which, along with lower literacy rates in the developing world, means that copy is less likely to be legible) or effective.

As a result, color and primary visuals need to work harder to delineate varieties and illustrate product benefits. And while it's true that incomes and modern trade are growing in places such as China, these varying packaging structures are unlikely to change. That's because these differences are driven by more than economics and retail channels. They are also impacted by regulations, sourcing options and functional needs often tied to storage and usage realities.

The net is that any global design system must be tailored to work across a wide range of retail formats. Mandating a "template" without appropriate adaptation is very likely to result in packaging that doesn't work on shelf or, for that matter, in the home.

Any global design system must be tailored to work across a wide range of retail formats such as high-frequency stores, which dominate many of the world's largest markets.

Local Tastes

Just as packaging structures must vary to meet local needs, graphic elements must also adapt. A single "look" or visual image is rarely compelling on a global level.

In part, it's because perceptions of beauty, health and appetite appeal differ widely by country. Certainly, walking down the chips (or "crisps") aisle in the UK, where you find shrimp-flavored potato chips, confirms the fact that flavor preferences vary culturally.

On a deeper and more challenging level, there are also regional differences in design aesthetics. While there's always a risk in over-generalizing, it's fair to say that Northern Europeans tend to be more receptive to simple, minimalist designs, which are often interpreted as sleek and sophisticated. The Chinese are used to busier packaging and tend to associate simple, understated packages with lower-end, generic products. And Latinos tend to react more positively to bold packaging, with strong visuals and use of color.

Global design systems also need to be adaptable to different pack forms, some of which may leave less "real estate" for on-pack communication.

In addition, basic information needs may also vary by market. In developed markets, shoppers are often quite familiar with core products and brands, which may offer marketers more "permission" to have fun with design and, perhaps, to use humor to differentiate. But in developing markets, brand familiarity (and disposable income) is often more limited, creating a greater need for packaging to be more literal in illustrating key product information. In a recent study, for instance, abstract "people" visuals were far more effective in Europe than in Thailand.

There have also been varying reactions to the use of English and/or Western branding on global packaging. Predictably, in some countries or regions, foreign branding is a positive. But in others, that's certainly not the case, and the English copy serves only to clutter the packaging.

Given these differences, it's easy to see why designs don't always travel well across borders, and marketers and designers often emerge from research frustrated that they have different "winning options" in different markets.

Market Challenges

When companies seek to globalize packaging, they are typically starting from different market realities in different countries. This isn't just a question of varying "looks." It's often a larger question of different branding and packaging challenges.

For example, we recently worked with a client seeking to unify a home care brand, which had a leading position in the United States, with varying brand names, appearances and market shares across India, China, Indonesia and Brazil.

In the United States, where the brand was dominant, the emphasis was on maintaining equity and facilitating shopping among the brand's many products on shelf. In Brazil, where the brand was smaller, the primary need was for packaging to "break through shelf clutter," to drive awareness and consideration and differentiate from a larger competitor.

It's crucial to recognize the business context and the implications for packaging to be able to develop effective solutions. These situations and priorities vary by country, and if they are ignored in the pursuit of a global "look," marketers run the risk of designing to the lowest-common denominator and ending up with global mediocrity.

Overcoming Obstacles

Given these challenges and the inevitable political battles within organizations about global versus local decision-making, the obvious question is: "What can companies do to increase the odds of successful global packaging?"

To begin, start by realistically defining "global packaging." The idea of global uniformity is neither attainable nor desirable. If it is put forth as the incoming objective, the end result is likely to be frustration, internal conflict and a half-baked solution. However, if a global design effort is defined more realistically—respecting key core global equity elements (a brand logo or identity, for instance)—the likelihood of success is far higher.

Second, use packaging research to guide and evaluate initiatives. This starts with a solid upfront understanding of local markets. In particular, it's vital to understand the "retail realities" (store context, shelving, merchandising, competitive set, etc.) that impact the shopping process and the "in-home realities" that impact packaging storage and usage. By doing this homework upfront, via store visits and consumer ethnographies, brands can avoid major blunders.

Of course, consumer research should also play a role in the decision-making process to help brands get past local marketer's agendas or opinions. At the evaluation stage, it's important to marry global research methods and metrics with a local interpretation of findings. In terms of methodology, it's nearly always important to start at the shelf, because shelf-based metrics of visibility and shopability are the most predictive of in-market success.

As for interpretation, setting appropriate action standards is challenging but critical. Generally speaking, the primary benchmark should be the brand's current packaging (i.e., *Are we improving?*) and a realistic goal is to drive improvements in some markets, while maintaining parity with current packaging in others. Nearly all global design systems involve some form of compromise—it's nearly impossible to drive wins in all countries.

But that's where flexibility and local customization come in. The most successful global packaging systems are those that build in flexibility. They mandate a few core global "constants" and then give the regions the freedom to use their superior local knowledge to customize appropriately.

In some cases, it's simply a case of modifying claims or customizing a visual to speak more directly to local priorities or sensitivities. In others, it may mean changing the packaging structure or communication hierarchy to work more effectively in store. In either case, it's a matter of making sure that global packaging works effectively within each local market, where the battles and shoppers are won and lost.

How is China Different?

Insights for Connecting with the Chinese Shopper

Perception Research Services (PRS) has been conducting packaging and shopper research studies in China for over twenty years. Across many Chinese clients, categories, and cities, we have often heard variations of the same question:

How is packaging different in China, relative to our experience across the world?

With this reasonable and relevant question in mind, we'd like to share several observations about Chinese shoppers, stores and packages, and discuss their implications for developing effective packaging and "winning at retail."

Starting with the Commonalities

As the question above implies, it is tempting, and perhaps natural, to look first for the differences that distinguish China from other countries. However, we'd argue that marketers and agencies are best served by grounding themselves and their packaging development efforts in the common challenges that packaging faces across all markets. Specifically, whether in Beijing, Buenos Aires, or Boston, an effective packaging system must typically:

Chinese packs often feature a balance of global branding and Chinese messaging, which reflects marketers' attempts to leverage the power of global brands while also conveying relevance to Chinese shoppers.

- Break through retail clutter to create attention and recognition;

- Be easily shopable to help people quickly and accurately find the right product;

- Connect on a visceral level to engage and appeal to shoppers;

- Convey key information to differentiate from competition and ultimately close sale; and

- Perform on a functional level to work in store and within people's lives and homes.

Thus, these core "realities" serve as a good starting point or "checklist" for developing effective packaging in China or any country. However, this is not an argument for global uniformity in packaging. In fact, across brands, we typically find that a single global design used across many different markets is unlikely to meet all of these objectives. That is due to major variations across countries in shoppers, retail environments, and competitors, all of which are important to consider in a Chinese context.

Considering the Chinese Shopper

What is particularly notable or unique about Chinese shoppers?

Many full-length books have been dedicated to this subject and there are always limitations in generalizing and condensing, particularly across a country of China's size and diversity. With that said, we can offer a few observations, especially regarding younger and more affluent shoppers in Shanghai and other more developed Western cities.

- They are open to considering new products and very influenced by well known Western brands and design. Thus, packaging is far more than a vessel to protect and transport the product. It is often an explicit driver of product choice and in some categories, a vehicle for personal expression of status, prestige and luxury. Design is especially important for "gifting" items.

Chinese packs typically feature more copy claims than packs in other markets, as a "more is more" mentality permeates, as it does in many Asian markets.

- They are digital and technology-savvy. Thus, packaging often needs to be considered and developed in the larger context of the path-to-purchase, which may include online pre-planning or the use of mobile devices and digital content in-store. In cities like Shanghai, certain categories sell up to 50 percent of their products online on portals like Taobao.

- They can be very skeptical of product quality. Thus, packaging, particularly for foods and beverages, needs to provide key reassurances of ingredients, of sourcing, of quality, and so forth. In fact, when we recently reviewed our database, we found that across categories, Chinese shoppers consistently rated brands and packaging far lower than shoppers in other countries on dimensions such as "High quality" and "Brand I trust." This last point also speaks to an opportunity for global brands to be a source of trust, if they are properly managed and highlighted on Chinese packaging as a vehicle of quality reassurance.

Entering the Store

Beyond the shoppers themselves, a second important dimension to consider is the retail environment because the shelf context and competitive set has a direct impact on how people see and react to packaging. In other words, what "breaks through clutter" in one store may fail to do so in another. Here, the Chinese market presents many considerations and challenges, including:

Pronounced differences across cities. Across categories, the competitors and shelf sets in Shanghai will vary significantly from those in Guangzhou, Beijing, or Harbin, to a far greater degree than that seen in other countries, i.e., New York vs. Dallas, or perhaps Southern vs. Northern Italy.

A divide between Hypermarkets vs. Convenience or Traditional Trade. These different channels place varying demands on packaging, as

Chinese packaging needs to work across a wide range of retail contexts and competitive situations, which vary by city or region. Therefore, it is often wise to design with flexibility or customization in mind.

they link to different shopping experiences and mindsets, shelf sets, and pack forms or sizes.

The presence of in-aisle promoters. While these people can facilitate shopping, they also hold the potential to distract, and they significantly impact the shopping experience and the role of packaging.

Taken collectively, these points suggest that Chinese packaging needs to work across a wide range of contexts. Therefore, it is often wise to design with flexibility or customization in mind, so that designs can be modified to work within different situations and structures.

Focusing on the Pack

Finally, we looked at Chinese packaging itself and can share two general observations.

- Chinese packs typically feature more copy claims than packs in other markets. Overall, a "more is more" mentality in terms of violators, on-pack claims, and so forth, permeates, as it does in many Asian markets. Of course, much of this is driven by cultural norms and expectations. A very simple appearance tends to signal "basic" or "downscale" in China, whereas it may speak to "sophistication" in Scandinavia.

  However, there are challenges in practice, as cluttered packaging creates difficulty in the aisle. In fact, when we reviewed our database, one striking finding was that Chinese shoppers were typically taking much longer than people in other countries to find specific products in aisle. While this may be linked to limited familiarity with many new brands and products, we suspect that it is also driven by the overwhelming amount of copy on many packs. Clearly, there is certainly an opportunity and need to ensure that packaging better facilitates shopping, particularly in complex product categories such as health and beauty.

- Chinese packs often feature a balance of Chinese vs. global branding and messaging. Often, we see that packaging directly and visually reflects marketers' attempts to leverage the power of global brands, such as Budweiser, and Coca-Cola, for example, while also conveying relevance to Chinese shoppers. Here, it is difficult to generalize, as the right strategy, and thus the right on-pack branding strategy, often varies by brand. Still, we can offer the following reminder: It is important to remember that FMCG packs (e.g., skin care), are often very small and often considered very quickly—within 5 seconds. Thus, there is a danger in trying to say and do too much and compromising clarity. Marketers may be better served focusing on a single clear branding message on their packaging and leveraging other in-store elements, such as displays and promotions, to convey local relevance. Similarly, they are better off conveying key product information visually, via pictures and colors, rather than repeating information in multiple languages and unreadable type on a front panel.

To develop winning packaging, marketers need to understand the unique dynamics of the Chinese market, including the shoppers, the retail stores and the country's unique packaging challenges.

Driving Packaging Excellence in China

What can marketers do to help ensure effective Chinese packaging?

There is no single formula for success, but you can promote the likelihood of success by:

- Recognizing the consistent, global challenges facing nearly all packaging systems. These pillars can serve as a good foundation and consistent language for approaching all packaging initiatives.

- Factoring in the unique dynamics of the Chinese market. These dynamics are rooted in shoppers, retail stores, and packages and they link to specific challenges more common to China, such as reassuring shoppers of product quality, facilitating product selection, and addressing regional issues.

- Finally, companies can benefit substantially by instilling the right processes for packaging development and consumer research, which include:

  - Studying the retail context—stores and channels, shelving, promotion, and regional variation—at the outset of design efforts and building these retail realities into design briefs

  - Developing and screening new packaging ideas within the shelf context, to gauge if they are visually impactful and easily shopable.

  - Simulating and testing the introduction of new packaging on shelf, to see how shoppers react and behave rather than asking shoppers to compare options and become designers.

Marketers and designers that follow these "best practices," and invest the time and resources to understand the Chinese shopper and store, will be well-rewarded with packaging that drives sales and wins at retail.

Getting the Most from Eye-Tracking
Understanding Its Applications, Insights & Limitations

Over the past five years, there's been an explosion in the availability and use of eye-tracking in consumer research, for applications ranging from packaging and copy testing to web usability. This is clearly a positive development, as more marketers, designers and agencies have come to recognize and benefit from its added-value. However, broader deployment has also inevitably led to misuse and misinterpretation of findings, in some cases, a "backlash" against eye-tracking.

Nearly 40 years ago, PRS pioneered the use of eye-tracking in marketing communications research. Today, we conduct over 800 studies annually using this technology, primarily in the context of packaging and shopper studies. This chapter shares our perspective on the primary value of eye-tracking and offers several "best practices" for its effective use. In addition, we'll briefly discuss new applications, which are allowing companies to leverage eye-tracking in different contexts.

Traditionally, eye-tracking has been used as part of pre-testing new packaging, shelving and advertising systems.

The Added-Value (and Limitations) of Eye-Tracking

To apply eye-tracking effectively, it's best to start with a fundamental understanding of both its added-value and its limitations. In other words: What exactly can tracking eye movement tell us? What questions can it help us answer? Across the media we've studied, PRS has found that the answer is three-fold, as eye-tracking can document:

Visibility
Do people even see and notice a package on a cluttered shelf, a display in an enormous store, or a link on a cluttered web screen?

Engagement
Do these marketing efforts hold their attention, or are they quickly bypassed?

Viewing Patterns/Communication Hierarchy
Which specific elements or messages draw attention and are consistently seen and read (and which are frequently overlooked)?

These three dimensions provide important direction in terms of *when* eye-tracking is most likely to be valuable. Because eye-tracking measures visibility and engagement, it is typically most relevant in situations in which the marketer is buying "space" (such as an ad in a magazine or a package on a shelf) and attempting to capture a viewer's time and attention. In these media, the shopper or reader is in control.

- She can spend as much (or as little) time as desired and "check out" at any time.

- She can start where she wishes and control the viewing sequence or order.

- She may focus all her attention on a compelling visual and never even notice the branding nor engage with claims.

Conversely, we've found that eye-tracking typically offers *less* added-value in broadcast media (such as television and some forms of digital marketing), which have a clearly defined time frame and viewing sequence—for example, a 15-second TV spot, with a defined beginning, middle and end. In these contexts, eye-tracking may answer a specific question (i.e., *Did viewers ever see the logo and read the tagline?*), but this learning may offer limited insight, as communication can also happen verbally, via the voice-over. Regardless of media or application, it's also very important to understand the limitations of eye-tracking. As many have correctly pointed out, eye-tracking doesn't tell us whether someone likes a package or wants to buy the product inside. A hypothetical example would be the proverbial "pink polka-dotted" packaging: It would certainly stand out and get visual attention within the toothpaste aisle, for example, but this increased visibility wouldn't necessarily convert to more purchases. This reality—that the execution with the most visual impact is *not* necessarily the most effective—is sometimes cited as an argument against using eye-tracking. However, it is more accurate as a reminder that:

A. Percent Noted
B. Percent Noted in 4 Seconds
C. Percent Re-Examined

Eye-tracking can be used to document shelf visibility (*Do shoppers see the brand as they first consider the category?*) and package viewing patterns (*Are important on-pack messages consistently seen?*).

Eye-tracking should *not* generally be used in isolation.

> The learning and insight comes from understanding the linkage between visibility and other key metrics such as brand recognition, message delivery, and persuasion.

Attention is an important "hurdle" for marketing communication, but not an end in itself.

> While "unseen is unsold," visibility is only the first step towards purchase.

In fact, we've repeatedly found that the primary value of eye-tracking lies in helping marketers uncover *why* efforts aren't working:

- Are they getting lost in clutter and never creating an opportunity to sell?

- Are they being seen, but not leading people to key messages?

- Are they fully considered, but not persuasive?

A "breakdown" on any single dimension leads to failure, yet each has a very different implication and potential solution. When used properly, eye-tracking is more than an evaluative metric; it is a *diagnostic tool,* which uncovers limitations—and provides direction to marketers and creatives.

"Best Practices" for Effective Use

In addition to designing studies and interpreting findings correctly, researchers also need to ensure that they are gathering valid and meaningful data. In the context of studies including eye-tracking, this often involves focusing on what *not* to do or say.

Don't show multiple options

Many clients have an incoming pre-disposition to show individuals many different versions of packs, ads, or shelf sets, in order to see how changes in design will impact visibility and viewing patterns. However, we've found that when a person sees multiple variations of the same piece, it alters her behavior: Inevitably, she begins looking to see "what's changed" and this negatively impacts the underlying eye-tracking data. Thus, while showing materials within competitive "clutter" (a cluttered shelf, magazine, etc.) is a "best practice" for eye-tracking studies, each person should see only execution of the test brand (i.e., monadic study design).

Don't ask "why?"

It's even more tempting to ask people directly *why* they looked at some things—and ignored others. And certainly, if consumers are asked these questions, they will provide answers and describe logical explanations for their viewing patterns and behavior.

Unfortunately, these well-intentioned "answers" are likely to be misleading, because we know from experience that visibility is primarily physiological, rather than rational. In other words, humans are "hard-wired" to see a huge green color block of Fructis shampoo, regardless of our perceptions of the brand, because the packaging creates strong contrast with its surroundings. Similarly, within advertisements, web screens, or packages, readers' viewing patterns are dictated by the treatment and layout of elements, rather than readers' interest in them. Thus, while follow-up questioning (on messaging, branding, communication, persuasion, etc.) is a "best practice" for eye-tracking studies, direct questioning on viewing patterns is not recommended.

Eye-tracking studies are only as valid as the size and quality of the stimuli shown to shoppers.

Don't cut corners on stimuli

Any marketing communication study is only as "valid" as the quality of what's shown to consumers. With eye-tracking studies, having the right stimuli is particularly critical, because a primary objective is often to gauge visibility within a cluttered store, magazine, or roadside. Yet many eye-tracking units are designed to

track eye movement as people view computer monitors. This makes sense for web-based marketing efforts, since the materials may ultimately be viewed on a monitor. However, it becomes problematic (and misleading) when attempting to gauge the in-store visibility of a packaging or merchandising system and an 8-foot wide product category or 40-foot aisle is shown on a 20-inch monitor. In fact, our research-on-research suggests that a "best practice" is to show items at 80 percent or more of life size, in order to accurately document visibility and viewing patterns.

Don't rely on qualitative samples

As eye-tracking becomes a core component of validation studies (a set of visibility or attention measures against which new systems will be judged), there's an understandable desire to gather these metrics earlier in the development process. Marketers and designers now want to incorporate eye-tracking in the screening process, to identify new options that will break through clutter and gather insights and diagnostics to guide refinements prior to quantitative testing.

This is the right thought process, but it is also important to be aware of the limitations of qualitative base sizes. In our experience, we've found that 20 to 30 eye-tracking interviews can provide insight regarding primary viewing patterns (i.e., readers' start point and typical path through an advertisement or package) and identify possible concerns (i.e., *Is a key claim getting "lost" in this design?*). However, a study of this small scope is not valid to gauge overall visibility (i.e., *What percentage of people even saw our brand?*), which requires quantitative sampling. Don't confuse "eye-tracking" and click-streams.

Finally, it is important to distinguish between actual eye-tracking, which records viewing patterns, and other methods, which ask people to click on parts of packs or ads that they claim to have noticed or found compelling. Simply put, the latter approach is not an accurate measurement of visibility, but rather of claimed interest. In addition, because the eye is much faster than the hand and mouse, it does not consistently correlate with actual viewing behavior.

New Directions: Into the Store

In addition to wider use, the recent revolution has also brought eye-tracking technology into new applications and contexts. Two of the more exciting directions involve the retail environment.

Virtual eye-tracking

By linking eye-tracking technology with sophisticated virtual store environments, researchers can now leverage eye-tracking while pre-testing new approaches to in-store signage, displays, aisle configuration, category management, and product assortment. They can simulate new retail scenarios, show them to shoppers at nearly life-size without actually producing and placing materials in stores, and document their impact on visibility and purchase:

- Does a new approach increase a brand's retail visibility?

- Are in-aisle displays or signage getting attention?

- If so, do they convert to additional purchases?

Mobile eye-tracking

Via a pair of eye-tracking glasses, it's now possible to create a videotape of each person's exact viewing patterns in any context. Mobile eye-tracking is being used most frequently in store environments, to track shopping patterns and document engagement with displays, signage, and packaging. We've also found it quite valuable in helping marketers understand what influences the shopper's in-store journey and to improve point-of-sale marketing across different retail environments, such as club stores, convenience stores, and kiosks.

Through the Consumer's Eye

While eye-tracking is not actually a new research tool, its use is growing significantly, as marketers' recognize the value of seeing the world through consumers' eyes. However, it measures only a piece of the marketing puzzle and should be viewed as a "single measure" of success. In fact, eye-tracking's greatest source of value lies in its diagnostic insights, as a tool for understanding why and guiding enhancements to marketing efforts.

More importantly, as with any research tool, eye-tracking's validity and value are dependent on how well it is used, in terms of applications, study design, stimuli and analysis. Thus, while researchers should aggressively leverage eye-tracking, they also need to adhere to fundamental principles to ensure meaningful data and insights. By doing so, they will help create more effective marketing efforts that "break through clutter" and help their companies "win" in an increasingly cluttered and competitive world, where consumers' attention can't be taken for granted.

Mobile eye-tracking can document shoppers' viewing patterns and engagement with packs and displays within actual stores.

Getting to Why

Measuring Emotion in Packaging Research

Few would dispute that emotion plays an important role in shopping and packaging. In a world of overwhelming choice down every aisle, it's clear that shoppers can't consider all options or rely solely on rational, fact-based product comparisons. Instead, they need to sort through items quickly and the packages that "breakthrough" visually and make an immediate visceral connection are most likely to end up in the shopping cart. In addition, we all know that what shoppers say is often inconsistent with what they do, and that people often face barriers in verbalizing their true feelings such as the desire not to offend, or socially acceptable responses.

For these reasons, PRS has long relied mainly on behavioral measures, including eye-tracking, shopping and product findability exercises from shelf, rather than direct questioning, to assess new packaging systems. More recently, we've explored a variety of approaches, including neuroscience, facial coding and visual images, to bring emotional measurement to packaging research. In fact, over the past several years, we've conducted over 50 studies in which these measures have been gathered in addition to validated metrics of packaging effectiveness.

Emotional measurement tools can be most valuable in identifying specific on-pack visuals that resonate with (or frustrate) shoppers.

From these studies, we've learned a great deal about the strengths and limitations of different approaches to emotional measurement. However, in this chapter, our intent is not to promote a single methodology. Instead, we'll speak more broadly about the role of emotion in packaging and share our perspective on the "added-value" of emotional measurement and our suggestions for using it effectively.

The Role of Emotion

Before diving into the measurement of emotion, it's important to start by considering the role of emotion in a packaging and shopping context. Here, we can offer some perspective, based on our experience:

> It is important to realize that the range of emotion evoked by packaging is typically far narrower than that of advertising or digital content.

Generally speaking, still images on packs evoke less emotional response than moving images, *such as those in commercials, movie trailers, etc,* which can use content and sound to "tell a story." In addition, the reality is that shopping for many products, particularly weekly "staples" found in grocery, drug, and mass stores, is more functional and task-oriented than experiential, and thus, the strongest "emotion" is often frustration, when shoppers are confused or can't find their desired product. Also, packages are often constrained by their limited size and their need to deliver key product information such quantity and flavor.

> However, we've found that packaging and point-of-sale can connect with shoppers on an emotional level, typically via the use of powerful visual images, design elements, or promotional concepts.

Despite the limitations cited above, we've found many cases in which packages have spoken to shoppers on an emotional level, by:

- Provoking a laugh or a smile via humor.
- Linking to emotionally "richer" content, advertising, or promotions— Disney characters, etc.
- Speaking to personal relevance, often via user imagery.
- Connecting with other senses such as touch and smell.

As these points suggest, the key is identifying visual images or design elements that do resonate with shoppers, and finding ways to incorporate them within packaging, signage, or displays. Thus, our focus has been less on identifying "the most emotional package" and more on uncovering the most compelling puppy or mother-and-child visual, for example.

Applying Emotional Measurement: Three Applications & Brief Case Studies

Across studies, we've applied emotional measurement in a variety of different ways.

- As part of pre-design research, to inspire and guide exploration.
- As part of screening a range of new design directions.
- As part of on-shelf validation testing.

Three recent studies illustrate these applications, along with the types of insights gathered

Pre-Design/Equity Research

A PRS client recently used emotional measurement as part of a "baseline" assessment of a brand's current packaging, in order to confirm strengths and limitations versus the competition and identify opportunities for improvement.

As might be expected, the study reinforced the power of a familiar brand mark. However, the research also revealed more weaknesses in current packaging than were expressed verbally. Specifically, there were negative emotional reactions to various aspects of on-pack information delivery, including visual icons and less-prominent product claims. These reactions suggested either confusion *regarding their intended meaning,* or difficulty reading smaller print. Taken collectively, they spoke to a need to "clean up" and simplify the packs. In addition, we found that the food visual was prominent and abundant, yet unappealing, which signaled a need to re-explore this important design element.

Screening Research

A major retailer recently created a new "own-brand" of food products. As part of screening potential design directions, we included emotional measures that revealed several important insights regarding logo treatments and product descriptors. Specifically, we found that a scripted logo treatment for this new brand was visually impactful, but far less emotionally engaging to shoppers than a more traditional style. Similarly, a more concise product depiction drew more reaction than longer, more extensive approaches. These insights guided the development of a new visual identity that was later launched in market.

Validation Research

In the context of a larger on-shelf evaluation of a new packaging system for a leading brand of cookies, PRS gathered shoppers' emotional and cognitive reactions to both the current and proposed new design systems. While the proposed system met many primary design objectives, the emotional component revealed several opportunities for enhancement.

- The cookie visual on the proposed packaging didn't appear to be working very hard, as it drew neutral reaction, despite its prominence.

- A specific on-pack claim was driving negative emotional reactions, on both current and proposed packaging, although it was known to be a valued feature.

These negatives appeared to be driven by execution of the message, which was too jarring on the current packaging and too difficult to read on the proposed.

These insights led to significant refinements to both design elements prior to launch. The claim was made more legible, whereas the cookie visual was given more energy via flying chips visuals.

As these cases illustrate, we've found that emotional measures can be powerful diagnostic tools, which are most valuable in uncovering shoppers' reactions to specific design elements. It can help us identify particularly compelling approaches and elements that may inadvertently be driving negative reactions.

Emotional insights led to significant refinements in the new Chips Ahoy! packaging — and resulted in an improved version being launched into market.

Original

Launched version

Uncovering *Why?*

Uncovering negatives also highlights another important role of emotional measurement, which is helping us to understand *why* a design system is or isn't working. Here, we've found that this can often help us to discern the underlying factors driving poor performance.

- In a personal care product study, an on-shelf shopping exercise showed that a proposed design system was not working and emotional measures pointed to changes in cap color and on-pack messaging as the likely drivers.

- In a frozen food study, a proposed design system drove declines in imagery and purchase and we found that removing a familiar brand character from the packaging had a negative emotional impact.

- In a cereal study, we found that a brand's current packaging was not connecting emotionally with shoppers, most likely due to the absence of a compelling product visual,and was the probable driver of recent sales declines.

In these cases and others, the pattern is clear: On-shelf behavioral measures such as purchase patterns, tell us *which* packaging systems are working and emotional measures help us uncover *why*.

And while it's best to be cautious in generalizing across brands and categories, we have seen several consistent drivers of negative emotion.

- One observation is that many negative reactions appear to be linked to *complexity*. They are cases in which shoppers are being asked to work "too hard" to decipher packaging, due to small print or unclear messaging. This finding is consistent with PRS' historical experience, which suggests that "less is more" in packaging communication.

- We've also seen that it is critical to get the product visuals right, as seemingly minor changes can have a significant impact. For example, we've found that eliminating the rising steam from a hot entrée visual, or not properly executing the "cheese pull" on a frozen pizza, drove negative emotional reactions to the packages.

In addition to identifying which elements need to be fixed, we've also found that emotional approaches can often help point us in the right direction. In fact, in most cases, our studies have uncovered alternative approaches, including more appetizing food visuals and more relevant claim treatments, that were more compelling and were ultimately incorporated into new packaging.

Linking the Digital & Physical Shopping Experiences

Based on our experience to date, we can offer several guidelines to marketers and designers for incorporating emotional measurement within packaging studies.

- First and foremost, researchers should use emotional measurement in conjunction with other packaging research tools, *most notably, measures of on-shelf performance,* rather than as a replacement for them.

- Second, it can be misleading to think in terms of absolute measurement, i.e. "the most emotional design." Instead, the focus should be on understanding reactions to design elements and using this learning to optimize packaging and in-store activation.

- Finally, insights are most valuable if they are gathered early in the design process to uncover compelling images, messages, etc., rather than at the end of the process, when the primary objective is to validate and there are fewer opportunities to make fundamental changes.

Emotional measurement can offer a window to a greater understanding of shoppers' motivations and, ultimately, a path to better packaging. However, as with all research tools, careful consideration must be given to how it is interpreted, reported, and used. Marketers and designers that approach it as a diagnostic and exploratory tool, and a source of design inspiration, are likely to benefit from its value, and develop packaging that engages shoppers, makes an emotional connection. and closes the sale.

Making Packaging Work Online
Linking the Digital & Physical Shopping Experiences

"How does our packaging look and work online?" It is a question that we're hearing more often from our clients, in categories ranging from diapers to dog food. And certainly, it is a relevant issue, given the growing impact of web-based shopping, and shoppers' increasing tendencies to do "homework" online prior to visiting the store.

Packaging's Role in Online Shopping

With that thought in mind, Perception Research Services recently conducted a series of in-depth interviews to observe and discuss online shopping for health and beauty products—such as vitamins, OTC medications, cosmetics, and hair and skincare products. The research process included using *PRS Mobile Eye-Tracking* to document what these shoppers did—including what they saw and missed—as they went through typical online shopping trips. Afterward, we conducted follow-up interviews to better understand their thoughts and reactions.

Overall, we found that packaging plays a very important role in the web-based shopping experience, albeit in ways that vary somewhat from the brick-and-mortar world. This is due to several key factors:

Eye-tracking research reveals that most online shoppers rely on the package visual as the primary source for feature and benefit communication, as they consider and compare products online.

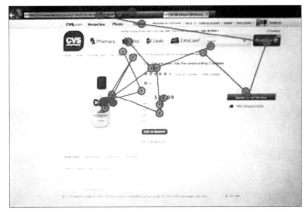

1. The different stages of the web-based shopping experience

Web-based shopping has several distinct phases (search and "de-selection," product comparison, selection, confirmation, and fulfillment) that place different demands on packaging.

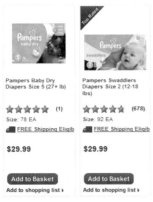

Pampers Baby Dry Diapers Size 5 (27+ lb)

⭐⭐⭐⭐⭐ (1)
Size: 78 EA
🚚 FREE Shipping Eligib

$29.99

Add to Basket
Add to shopping list ▸

Pampers Swaddlers Diapers Size 2 (12-18 lbs)

⭐⭐⭐⭐⭐ (678)
Size: 92 EA
🚚 FREE Shipping Eligib

$29.99

Add to Basket
Add to shopping list ▸

Huggies Pull-Ups Learning Designs Diapers 3T-4T Disney Princess

☆☆☆☆☆
Size: 50 EA
🚚 FREE Shipping Eligib

$23.99

Add to Basket
Add to shopping list ▸

Huggies Little Movers Diapers Size 4 (22-37 lb)

⭐⭐⭐⭐⭐ (8838)
Size: 56 EA
🚚 FREE Shipping Eligib

$23.99

Add to Basket
Add to shopping list ▸

Online shoppers typically rely on package thumbnails for brand identification and product confirmation, as they sort through a range of product options.

- In nearly all cases, the package is a vital tool in the search and "de-selection" process, as initial searches inevitably lead to a myriad of items to consider and online shoppers usually rely on packaging images for brand identification and product confirmation.

- Later, once shoppers form a smaller consideration set, the package also plays a central role in product and brand comparisons, which often take place across screens and websites. While the web allows for additional information delivery (beyond the pack), our eye-tracking research reveals that shoppers typically rely on the pack for the feature and benefit communication.

- Once shoppers place a product in an online shopping cart, we see them frequently double-checking the pack to confirm correct product selection, prior to the final purchase.

- Finally, with online shopping, packaging also plays an important role in the fulfillment process. When the product arrives at home, the packaging reassures the shopper that it is genuine (not a knock-off). Thus, in addition to providing product protection, the outer shipping container can be valuable as a branding and marketing vehicle. In fact, it can also add value to the online shopping experience by sharing additional information, product samples, etc.

2. The lack of shelf context

In some ways, the package may be more critical online, because there's a more level playing field than in physical stores: Both big and small brands are typically represented by one SKU—and larger brands find it harder to create billboards that dominate shoppers' attention and become self-fulfilling in maintaining their category leadership.

In addition, because web-based shoppers typically see only one SKU at a time (rather than a larger brand at shelf), they often struggle to find a particular variant within a line (form, formulation, scent, etc.). In fact, we find that some shoppers simply purchase the first variant they encounter, without realizing it isn't their usual variety.

3. The lack of tactile interaction

Because shoppers can't physically pick up packages—and small packages often look similar to larger ones in an online context—shoppers have difficulty gauging product quantity, particularly when quantity information is not always readily apparent. Predictably, this sometimes leads to price/value concerns, as shoppers focus on price alone.

Five Principles for Online Success

Given the uniqueness of the online shopping context, marketers and designers will be well-served to keep several core objectives in mind as they develop and adapt their packaging for the web:

1. Foster brand recognition. Create a distinctive and memorable set of visual equities, via the package shape, color and graphic elements, to foster immediate brand recognition online.

2. Support a high quality impression. Use high-resolution digital images of the package, to promote a high quality impression of the brand and product. Also, remember to display the packaging (primary and secondary) that is most important to shoppers.

3. Clearly convey quantity. Use simple and legible copy, particularly related to size or quantity to ensure the right price/value perception.

Packaging also plays an important role in the fulfillment process, as it can provide brand reassurance and add value through additional information, product samples and promotions.

4. Facilitate product comparisons. Find ways to quickly show the relevant product range, so as to help shoppers pick the right product for them.

5. Add value with the shopper. Use the outer container to provide brand reassurance and add value to the fulfillment stage.

By following these principles and understanding the online shopper, companies can help avoid potential barriers to purchase, create stronger synergy between online and in-store efforts, and position themselves to "win at retail" in this growing channel.

Connecting with Hispanic Shoppers
New Insights from Eye-Tracking Research

At Perception Research Services, we regularly conduct research studies with Hispanic shoppers, in both English and Spanish and across a variety of locations, including actual stores, PRS Retail Labs, via the web, etc. Often, we're asked to share insights for effective shopper marketing with this growing segment, on issues ranging from multi-lingual labeling to compelling new product offerings, and appropriate imagery and messaging for in-store displays. Of course, there is always a danger in generalizing, particularly about a population this diverse in background, demographics, and socio-economics. However, we can relate several themes and observations that have emerged consistently across studies and product categories, and speak to their implications for connecting with Hispanics.

Many Hispanic shoppers cite social considerations and sensual factors (such as scent and softness) as key purchase drivers. Thus, it is important to connect with them on a visceral level in the aisle.

The Generation Gap

In many studies of Hispanics, much is made of the important differences in background and culture among Puerto Ricans, Dominicans, Mexicans, etc. Certainly, these distinctions are real and they can impact how marketers reach and speak with specific sub-segments of the Hispanic market.

However, In our experience, we've repeatedly encountered a more dramatic "generation gap":

- 1st Generation Hispanics are often looking for reminders of their native country and thus, they usually find comfort in familiar brands.

- 2nd and 3rd Generation Hispanics are often more eager to define themselves as part of the larger American society. Although they respect their heritage, they are typically more open to experimentation and thus seek brands that are different from "their Mama's and Abuelita's brand."

Recently, we observed this dynamic in the laundry care aisle, as a leading brand, of Mexican origin, was beloved by a core group of loyal and aging shoppers, yet far less compelling to younger, more assimilated Hispanic shoppers.

Clearly, this dynamic is not unique to Hispanics. In some sense, it plays out across nearly all immigrant groups. Nonetheless, the generation gap has important implications for marketing to these shoppers. In particular, it creates challenges for historically Hispanic brands, such as Goya, Jaritos, and Masa, as they look to expand and speak to new audiences. These brands also face a difficult balancing act in leveraging their heritage and retaining their loyal customers, while also attracting a new generation of Hispanic shoppers. In fact, we've found that creating compelling sub-brands is a more effective strategy than attempting to dramatically "contemporize" brands that are linked to comfort and tradition.

The Acculturation Gap

Closely aligned with the Generation Gap is an Acculturation Gap, which speaks to Hispanic shoppers' comfort level with English and has a dramatic impact on their shopping patterns.

Consistently, we've seen that *More Acculturated* Hispanic shoppers, i.e., those more fluent in English, largely mirror the General Population across key dimensions of shopping behavior, including:

- Time spent within different product categories.
- Perceptions of product categories, ease or difficulty of shopping, etc.
- Purchase patterns, quantities, brand preferences, etc.

Conversely, *Less Acculturated* Hispanic shoppers, whose dominant language is Spanish:

- Spend significantly less time in the aisle.
- Are less likely to actively compare brands or products.
- Are less likely to see and engage with POS materials.
- Are more likely to purchase "their regular brand."

What's happening is quite clear and logical: Less Acculturated Hispanic shoppers are often overwhelmed by the multitude of product choices in the aisle, most of which are presented in English. Thus, they "default to the familiar" and head straight for familiar colors, shapes and icons.

PRS Eye-Tracking reveals that Less Acculterated Hispanic shoppers spend less time considering packages and are less likely to engage with specific on-pack messages, most likely because they have "trained themselves" to shop visually.

In fact, in a recent oral care study, our *PRS Mobile Eye-Tracking* videos repeatedly documented this behavior, as Less Acculturated shoppers went straight for the familiar "red wall" of Colgate, without even pausing to consider a multitude of other options.

Interestingly, we've seen that this pattern extends to packaging consideration as well. In our eye-tracking studies, we typically find that Less Acculturated Hispanic shoppers spend significantly less time than the General Population considering individual packages, and they are far less likely to read specific on-pack claims.

This reality brings into question the common strategy of adopting multi-lingual packaging, in an attempt to appeal to Hispanic shoppers. Across brands and categories, we've found that multi-lingual

labeling rarely has a major positive influence on Hispanic shoppers. In fact, if executed poorly, it can have a negative impact, by creating excess clutter and detracting from packaging appeal. That is because these multi-lingual packs are trying to communicate via copy, albeit in Spanish, to people who have "trained themselves" to shop almost entirely by color, iconography, and visual imagery. To be clear, this is not necessarily an argument against incorporating Spanish messaging on packs. However, if they pursue a multi-lingual strategy, marketers should be careful to:

- Minimize front-of-pack copy, in favor of visual icons or images, when possible.
  For example, a visual of a strawberry is more effective than saying "Strawberry" or "Fresa" in several languages.

- Group more detailed Spanish copy together, on the back of a package.
  Create a "Spanish section" with key information, rather than repeating claims in multiple languages.

- Use POS materials
  Often, POS displays provide more space and "real estate" than packaging for messages and visual images that connect emotionally and convey personal relevance to Hispanic shoppers.

We've found that multi-lingual labeling rarely has a major positive influence on Hispanic shoppers – and if not executed properly, it can have a negative impact, by creating excess clutter and detracting from packaging appeal.

This last point, on connecting emotionally and appealing to the senses, is particularly relevant, as Hispanic shoppers are often quite open in referring to social considerations as a primary driver of their purchase decisions. This quote from an oral care shopper is quite representative:

"Teeth are an important factor in a person. They talk a lot about a person, if they don't have clean teeth and good oral hygiene . . ."

Across categories, we've consistently seen and heard references to more visceral, sensual factors, such as scent and softness, as decision drivers among Hispanic shoppers. Indeed, we've documented that Hispanic shoppers are more likely than General Population to open packages, if necessary, to smell and touch products before making purchases.

Connecting & Persuading in the Aisle

How can marketers apply these insights to communicate more effectively with Hispanic shoppers?

As a starting point, they need to ground their efforts in the understanding that the shopping experience for Less Acculturated Hispanic shoppers is primarily visual, visceral. and habitual, rather than purely rational. Faced with a vast array of product choices, typically presented in English, these customers typically use familiar colors, shapes, and icons to navigate towards familiar, and thus "safe," choices. To succeed in this world, brands need to:

Leverage visual equities

If you are fortunate enough to own "Tide Orange" or "Fructis Green," this asset should be managed carefully and exploited fully. One powerful strategy is to use a solid brand block to create a "beacon" in the aisle, which leads Hispanic shoppers immediately to "their brand" and facilitates shopping, by reducing a 40-foot aisle to a more manageable 6-8 foot "mini-section". Alternatively, strong displays can serve a similar purpose, by visually pre-empting competition and allowing shoppers to avoid the hassle of the in-aisle experience.

Because many Less Acculterated Hispanics head straight for familiar colors, shapes and icons, marketers can benefit by creating strong brand blocks that leverage visual equities.

For smaller brands or new products, the key is to create strong visual equities, via distinctive and "ownable" colors, shapes, and icons, in order to avoid "blending into the clutter"of the category. Kraft's Mio serves as a positive example, as its unique shape and design language created visual breakthrough and a very recognizable icon for Hispanic shoppers to quickly and easily find in the aisle.

Keep it simple

Less Acculturated Hispanic shoppers have largely trained themselves to shop visually, rather than relying on words. Marketers should accommodate this reality, by using alternative color codes and pack structures rather than copy to differentiate among products and varieties and facilitate shopping. This philosophy also applies to on-pack communication, as a compelling visual typically has more impact than a written claim. While copy and claims do have a role, "less is more" should be the guiding philosophy. A strong, clear singular message, in English or Spanish, is far more likely to be seen, read, and acted upon, than a multitude of claims in small print, which discourage engagement and can detract from clarity and appeal.

Connect emotionally

In-store signage and displays should be viewed as opportunity to gain visual attention—"break through clutter"—to facilitate shopping and to send a powerful message that connects with Hispanic shoppers on a visceral and personal level. Often, this last challenge is a matter of uncovering underlying purchase drivers such as beauty, social acceptance, love of family, etc., and finding a compelling and ownable way to convey this visually. Alternatively, this can involve a way to engage with the brand on a more visceral and sensorial manner, via tasting, touching, or smelling.

Start with the shopper & store

Finally, it is important to remember that effective packaging and shopper marketing programs are rooted in an understanding of both the shopper and the retail context. And while we've discussed several underlying dynamics impacting Hispanic shoppers, it is also important to "visit" their shopping environment. Of course, the reality is that Hispanic people shop at many different stores and it is an anachronism at best to assume that all or most Hispanics are shopping at bodegas. But with that said, it would also be a mistake to ignore the role of these small, cluttered stores and their shopkeepers, particularly among Less Acculturated shoppers. And one visit to a bodega or a cluttered Walmart or Dollar Store, with overstocked shelves, poor lighting, and packages turned sideways, is an excellent reminder that products are not always presented as they were intended. Thus, we need to design for these "retail realities" and ensure that packaging is recognizable and shopable from all angles, and that POS is working to properly highlight products, rather than adding to clutter and confusion.

If these four principles are somewhat familiar and universal in nature, this is by intent. That's because the core strategies for effective marketing to Hispanics are more generally applicable. As shoppers, we all face an overwhelming amount of choice in the store, and we all use visual cues to sort through this stimuli and quickly find trusted brands and familiar products. With Less Acculturated Hispanic shoppers, this process is simply accentuated, given their language barriers. So if marketers can use design—colors, shapes, symbols, images—to effectively break through clutter, simplify shopping, and connect emotionally with these shoppers, the same lessons can be applied to help brands "win at retail" across a wider range of shoppers and stores.

When targeting Hispanic shoppers, it is important to understand and design for the "retail realities" of the cluttered bodega environment.

Historically Hispanic brands such as Goya face a difficult balancing act as they look to remain relevant for 2nd and 3rd generation Hispanic shoppers.

Acknowlegements

I would like to thank my colleagues at PRS, many of whom have contributed greatly to these articles. A special thanks to Jonathan Asher and Vincenzo Ciummo, who have acted as both co-authors and editors, and especially to Janice Lai, who has worked tirelessly (and very effectively) in bringing this book to life.

I'd also like to extend a thank you to Doris Walsh, Jim Madden, and Anne Kilgore, the team at Paramount Market Publishing, for their input and collaboration.

visible
|
legible
|
comprehendable
|
desirable
|
actionable